complete

griddling

complete
griddling

Fran Warde

hamlyn

This edition first published in the U.K. in 1999 by
Hamlyn, a division of Octopus Publishing Group Limited
2–4 Heron Quays, London E14 4JP

Reprinted 2001

Copyright © 1999, 2001 Octopus Publishing Group Limited

ISBN 0 600 60559 0

Printed in China

NOTES
Both metric and imperial measurements have been given in all
recipes. Use one set of measurements only, and not a mixture
of both.

Standard level spoon measurements are used in all recipes.
1 tablespoon = one 15 ml spoon
1 teaspoon = one 5 ml spoon

Eggs should be medium to large unless otherwise stated.
The Department of Health advises that eggs should not be
consumed raw. This book contains dishes made with raw or lightly
cooked eggs. It is prudent for more vulnerable people such as
pregnant and nursing mothers, invalids, the elderly, babies and
young children to avoid uncooked or lightly cooked dishes made
with eggs. Once prepared, these dishes should be kept
refrigerated and used promptly.

Meat and poultry should be cooked thoroughly. To test if poultry
is cooked, pierce the flesh through the thickest part with a skewer
or fork — the juices should run clear, never pink or red. Do not re-
freeze poultry that has been frozen previously and thawed.
Do not re-freeze a cooked dish that has been frozen previously.

Milk should be full fat unless otherwise stated.

Nut and Nut Derivatives
This book includes dishes made with nuts and nut derivatives. It is
advisable for customers with known allergic reactions to nuts and
nut derivatives and those who may be potentially vulnerable to
these allergies, such as pregnant and nursing mothers, invalids,
the elderly, babies and children to avoid dishes made with nuts
and nut oils. It is also prudent to check the labels of pre-prepared
ingredients for the possible inclusion of nut derivatives.

Pepper should be freshly ground black pepper unless otherwise
stated.

Fresh herbs should be used, unless otherwise stated. If
unavailable, use dried herbs as an alternative, but halve the
quantities stated.

Measurements for canned food have been given as a standard
metric equivalent.

Ovens should be pre-heated to the specified temperature — if
using a fan-assisted oven, follow the manufacturer's instructions
for adjusting the time and the temperature.

Vegetarians should look for the 'V' symbol on a cheese to ensure
it is made with vegetarian rennet. There are vegetarian forms of
Parmesan, feta, Cheddar, Cheshire, Red Leicester, dolcelatte and
many goats' cheeses, among others.

Contents

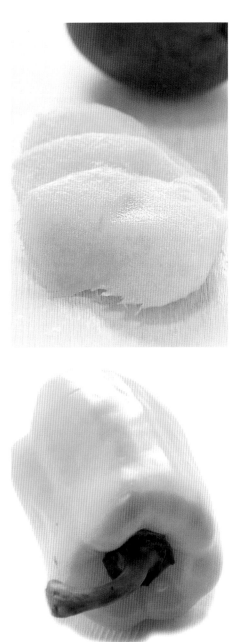

Introduction

Griddling is a popular new trend in cooking. It is incredibly versatile, as well as being great fun and simple to do. A griddle pan looks like a frying pan with a ridged base (see page 30) and is used on top of the stove. Once you have bought a griddle pan and had some practice, you will find griddling an effortless and really enjoyable way of preparing food, and your pan will become an integral part of the kitchen.

Successful griddling recreates the look and taste of food cooked over an outdoor barbecue, giving griddled ingredients a delicious smoky barbecued flavour. It can be used for virtually any type of food, encompassing a wide range of ingredients with different origins – particularly seafood, red and white meat, vegetables, fruit and some cheeses. The variety of dishes that can be cooked in a griddle pan certainly adds to its appeal.

Griddles have been designed for cooking ingredients without the need to add oil or fat. This makes griddling a fat-free and moisture-retaining way of cooking – a popular notion with health-conscious cooks. Not only is it a healthy method, it is a fast one, too – something of particular relevance to busy cooks today.

The griddling process

The griddle pan should always be heated through before you start to cook. This should be done over a moderate to high heat so that it can heat up evenly, and will take 2–3 minutes. To test whether the griddle is hot enough,

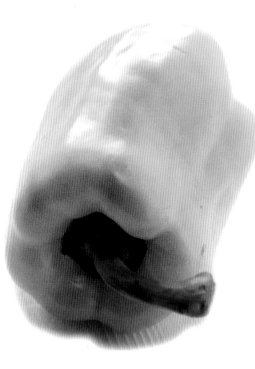

'Successful griddling recreates the look and taste of food cooked over an outdoor barbecue, giving griddled ingredients a delicious smoky barbecued flavour, ...'

splash a few drops of water on the surface; they should sizzle violently and immediately evaporate. If they do not, continue heating the pan for a little longer. Alternatively, hold your hand about 2.5 cm/1 inch above the surface of the griddle, taking care not to burn it. If it feels hot, the griddle is ready for cooking.

When sufficiently preheated, a griddle pan acts like a branding iron when food is first placed on it, and gives the food its characteristic chargrilled stripes, which enhance its flavour. Thereafter, the food on the griddle cooks at a steady, consistent heat, and it is sometimes necessary to turn down the heat a little to achieve this. Besides giving food the appetizing chargrilled effect, the ridges on the bottom of the pan also raise the food slightly, so that it does not sit in its own juices. The air space between the ridges creates steam and gives the food some breathing space.

Food will stick to the griddle when first put on it, but once it has seared and a crust has formed, it can be moved or turned over. If the food still sticks when you come to turn it, it is often best to leave it a little longer. This is particularly true for griddled fish, polenta, fish cakes or burgers – if you try to turn these too quickly they will stick to the pan or fall apart. The secret is not to have the heat under the griddle so high that the food burns on the outside but remains raw on the inside. If you are cooking foods that are quite fatty, you may need to drain off the fatty juices occasionally.

Tips for successful griddling

Once you start griddling, everything happens quite quickly so make sure you have all your ingredients to hand.

Since griddling recipes tend to involve relatively few ingredients, the quality of these ingredients is crucial and influences the final flavour. The emphasis is therefore on crisp vegetables and fruit, and fresh meat and seafood. Do experiment with griddling recipes to discover your favourites but a useful tip is to keep it simple. If you use too many ingredients, nothing will stand out and the simple perfection of griddling will be lost.

Not only do better-quality ingredients have more flavour, but they will cook more quickly in the pan. Thin and relatively tender foods are best suited to griddling – foods that are no more than 5 cm/2 inches thick work best as the centre will cook before the outside becomes dry and overcooked. Thicker cuts of chicken or pork, for example, can be seared on the griddle and then moved to a preheated oven to cook all the way through.

Once cooked, serve griddled food with just a squeeze of lemon or lime juice or a drizzle of oil over the top, or take a look at the recipes below. The choice of accompaniments, marinades and sauces can make griddling as simple or as spectacular as you like.

Wet marinades

A wet marinade is a liquid in which food is steeped. It is usually made with oil, seasoning and an acidic liquid such as lemon juice, vinegar, wine, yogurt or pulped tomatoes. Marinate food in a non-reactive dish – that is, one made of glass or ceramic – which holds the food snugly in a single layer. Sealable heavy-duty plastic bags are also an option for marinating. Any leftover marinade can be refrigerated in a covered jar for several weeks.

It is best not to put salt in marinades for meat as it draws out the juices and dries out the meat. Instead, season griddled meat just before or after cooking.

Red wine marinade

150 ml/¼ pint red wine
2 tablespoons lemon juice
1 onion, thinly sliced
1 carrot, thinly sliced
1 celery stick, finely chopped
sprig of parsley
sprig of thyme
1 bay leaf
6 black peppercorns, bruised
1 garlic clove, crushed

Combine all the ingredients in a large bowl and leave to stand for about 1 hour before adding to red meat to be marinated.

Citrus marinade

finely grated rind and juice of 1 orange or
 lemon, or 2 limes
1 tablespoon dark soy sauce
3 teaspoons clear honey
1 cm/½ inch piece of fresh root ginger, peeled
 and finely chopped
pepper

Combine the ingredients together in a jug and use for marinating pork, chicken or oily fish before griddling.

Marinades

Certain cuts of meat and fish benefit greatly from being marinated for a while before cooking. Marinades can be as simple as olive oil with a splash of lemon juice, perhaps with a little added yogurt, or they can be more heavily flavoured with garlic, chillies, other spices or honey.

Marinades are certainly marvellous for preserving moisture and enhancing the flavour of many griddled meats and fish – and even vegetables and fruit – but their use in tenderizing is not as effective as once thought. While acidic marinade ingredients will tenderize the surface of meat after a period of time, they have no effect on connective tissue, which means that the inner flesh will have not been improved at all.

Although recipes often stipulate a length of time for marinating, this is rarely critical and food can be marinated for longer or shorter, as convenient. It makes no difference whether a marinade, for example a flavoured oil, that is being used only to moisten food or as an external seasoning is added to food just before cooking or hours in advance. However, the longer that a marinade intended to change the flavour or texture of food is in place, the greater will be the effect – allow 4–24 hours. Foods marinating for 1– 2 hours or less can be left out at room temperature; otherwise marinating should take place in the refrigerator. It is best to allow the food to warm to room temperature (this takes about 30 minutes) before griddling. Drain off the marinade and blot the food to remove any excess liquid. Also, brush off larger marinade particles such as chopped onion, fresh herbs or garlic from the meat or fish since these will burn. Near the end of cooking, brush or sprinkle these marinade particles on the food if you like. Burned-on food residue can ruin the taste of the best ingredients, so be sure to clean the pan thoroughly after each use, following the instructions specific to your pan.

'...There are many bottled sauces available but few beat making your own...'

Dry marinades

A dry marinade is a paste made from a blend of spices and dried or fresh herbs, which can be massaged into meat, poultry or fish. The concept is to imbue the food with your chosen blend, which will become stronger the longer it is left. The herbs and spices explode with flavour as they cook and form a delicious crusty exterior to the food.

Before applying a dry marinade, rinse or wipe clean the food to be marinated and blot dry with kitchen paper. Lightly oil all surfaces, then massage the spice rub into the food. Depending on the type of spice mixture, use 1–2 tablespoons per 500 g/1 lb of meat, poultry or fish. Let the food stand for 1 hour at room temperature before cooking to allow the spices to permeate the flesh.

There are many commercial spice combinations available but try making your own. A dry marinade made with fresh herbs and spices will keep in the refrigerator, if tightly covered, for up to three days. One made with dried seasonings can be stored in an airtight container for several weeks.

Sauces, pestos and butters

Since griddling usually involves adding no additional liquid or oil to the ingredients being cooked, various salsas (see pages 74, 166 and 230) and sauces, both hot and cold, are the perfect accompaniment to griddled food. Such accompaniments tend to reflect regional influences and individual taste. There are many bottled sauces available but few beat making your own. This is particularly evident with home-made mayonnaise and pestos, which taste very different from the commercial variety and can be made in seconds in a food processor or blender. (See also Aïoli, page 64).

Classic mayonnaise

1 egg yolk
2 teaspoons lemon juice
1 teaspoon Dijon mustard
pinch of sugar
250–300 ml/8–10 fl oz extra virgin olive oil
sea salt and pepper

1 Place the egg yolk, lemon juice, mustard, sugar and salt and pepper in a blender or food processor and process for 30 seconds until pale in colour.

2 With the motor running, add the oil in a very thin but steady stream through the funnel, until the sauce is thick and glossy. Thin with a little boiling water, if necessary, to achieve a softer consistency.

Variation: Add an extra ingredient to the mayonnaise, such as finely chopped basil or watercress or a spoonful of mustard, for a different flavour.

Fresh tomato sauce

1 kg/2 lb ripe tomatoes, roughly chopped
2 tablespoons extra virgin olive oil
2 garlic cloves, chopped
2 tablespoons chopped basil
1 teaspoon grated lemon rind
pinch of sugar
sea salt and pepper

1 Place all the ingredients in a large saucepan and bring to the boil. Cover and simmer over a gentle heat for 30 minutes.

2 Remove the lid and cook for a further 20 minutes until the sauce is thick. Adjust the seasonings to taste and use as required.

Variation: Use 2 x 400 g/14 oz cans of chopped tomatoes in place of the fresh tomatoes, but simmer for only 10 minutes instead of 30 minutes.

Pestos

Pesto sauces are ideal served with griddled vegetables or fish in particular (see pages 40, 92 and 196). The secret of a good pesto is the freshness of the garlic. Pesto is very adaptable and you can experiment with different versions of the recipe below to create pestos with different textures and flavours. Try using blanched almonds, cashews, pistachios, hazel nuts or walnuts instead of the usual pine nuts, which may be plain or toasted (see page 40). Replace the basil with other herbs, such as parsley, dill, sorrel or rocket; or use a doubled quantity of soft goats' cheese in place of the hard cheese.

Classic pesto sauce

1 garlic clove, crushed
25 g/1 oz pine nuts
25 g/1 oz basil leaves
75 ml/3 fl oz extra virgin olive oil
2 tablespoons freshly grated Parmesan or
  pecorino cheese
sea salt and pepper

Place the garlic, pine nuts and basil in a blender and process until fairly smooth, or grind them together using a pestle and mortar. Gradually beat in the oil, then stir in the Parmesan or pecorino and adjust the seasoning to taste.

Variation: For a Red Pesto, add 50 g/2 oz drained and sliced sun-dried tomatoes in oil to the above ingredients and blend to a rough paste. For an even stronger flavour, substitute half the oil from the sun-dried tomato jar for half the olive oil in the recipe.

'Once you start griddling, everything happens quite quickly so make sure you have all your ingredients to hand...'

Savoury butters

A savoury, or compound, butter is a blend of butter and herbs, spices or other seasonings. When placed on top of griddled fish, meat and vegetable dishes at the time of serving, it melts to form an instant, glossy sauce (see pages 122 and 162).

Herb butters are scrumptious and very simple to make. The basic recipe for Herb Butter below can be varied, according to what herbs you have available. The butter should be cool and firm but not taken straight from the fridge.

Herb butter

75 g/3 oz butter
1 garlic clove, peeled
3 tablespoons chopped parsley or
  2 tablespoons chopped basil, mint or tarragon
1 tablespoon lemon juice
sea salt and pepper

Process the butter in a blender to soften or pound it using a pestle and mortar until it is creamy, then add all of the other ingredients and mix well. Chill until firm.

Ginger and herb butter

75 g/3 oz butter
1½ teaspoons grated fresh root ginger
1 teaspoon grated orange rind
1 tablespoon orange juice
1 teaspoon clear honey
1½ tablespoons chopped chervil
sea salt and pepper

Make up the Ginger and Herb Butter, following the same method as for Herb Butter. Serve with griddled fish fillets, such as salmon or monkfish, or griddled baby carrots.

Thyme butter

75 g/3 oz butter
3 tablespoons chopped thyme
3 teaspoons grated lemon rind
½ teaspoon cayenne pepper
½ teaspoon sea salt

Melt the butter in a small saucepan and fry the thyme, lemon rind, cayenne pepper and salt over a gentle heat for 2–3 minutes until softened. Leave to infuse for about 30 minutes before using dotted over griddled food, such as baby courgettes, lamb chops or sea bass fillets.

Salads

Pear and Pecorino Salad

This makes a great summertime salad, and the combination of the pears and hard Pecorino cheese is pure bliss.

Serves: **4**

Preparation time: 10 minutes

Cooking time: 2–4 minutes

4 pears, peeled
250 g/8 oz rocket
4 tablespoons olive oil
2 tablespoons balsamic vinegar
150 g/5 oz Pecorino cheese
sea salt and pepper

1 Heat the griddle pan. Cut the pears into 4 and core the quarters, then slice each quarter in half. Place on the griddle and cook for 1–2 minutes on each side.

2 Place the rocket in a bowl with the olive oil, balsamic vinegar and a little salt and pepper and toss well.

3 Using a vegetable peeler, peel the Pecorino into long ribbons and add to the rocket. Arrange on 4 individual plates and place the griddled pears on top. Serve immediately.

FOOD FACT • Pecorino is a hard Italian cheese, made from sheep's milk, which is used in much the same way as Parmesan. It has a strong salty taste, and is white to pale yellow in colour.

Griddled Potato and Spinach Salad with Mint Dressing

Serves: **4**

Preparation time: 10 minutes

Cooking time: 45 minutes

750 g/1½ lb new potatoes
4 tablespoons Greek yogurt
1 bunch of mint, chopped
1 garlic clove, crushed
100 g/3½ oz baby spinach leaves
sea salt and pepper

1 Heat the griddle pan. Cut the potatoes in half lengthways and place some on the griddle to cook on each side for 10 minutes. Repeat until all the potatoes are cooked and soft. Place in a large bowl, set aside and keep warm.

2 Place the Greek yogurt in a small bowl. Add the chopped mint, the garlic and a little seasoning; mix well.

3 Place the spinach leaves in the griddle pan and cook, using two spoons to move the spinach around in the griddle. Cook for 3–4 minutes so that it is just wilting.

4 Add the spinach and the minty yogurt to the potatoes. Mix well and serve immediately.

FOOD FACT • With their delicious, almost peppery taste, tender young spinach leaves are particularly versatile; when used raw they are almost squeaky to bite. Fresh spinach leaves can be bought prewashed and ready for use. If you are washing spinach yourself, wash the leaves well in a bowl of water, changing the water several times to remove the grit that spinach often contains.

Griddled Mushroom and Watercress Salad

The contrasting textures of the griddled field mushrooms and the fresh watercress add to the appeal of this recipe, and the combination works well with the soft creamy goats' cheese on griddled bread.

Serves: **4**

Preparation time: 10 minutes

Cooking time: 25 minutes

4 slices of country bread
4 large flat field mushrooms
125 g/4 oz goats' cheese
3 tablespoons olive oil
1 tablespoon cider vinegar
125 g/4 oz watercress
sea salt and mixed peppercorns, crushed

1 Heat the griddle pan. Place the bread on the pan and griddle for 1–2 minutes on each side until browned.

2 Place the mushrooms on the griddle, gills down, and cook over a medium heat for 10 minutes. Turn the mushrooms over and cook for another 10 minutes. (The undersides are cooked first to seal in all the juices.)

3 Place the griddled bread on 4 individual plates and spread each slice with some goats' cheese. Mix together the olive oil, vinegar and seasoning in a small jug to make a dressing.

4 When the mushrooms are cooked, remove from the griddle pan and slice. Mix them and their juices with the watercress and prepared dressing and heap on to the prepared bread. Serve immediately.

Moroccan Griddled Vegetable Salad

Try making this salad in advance so that all the flavours can blend. Leave it, covered, at room temperature for up to 5 hours. This makes a good accompaniment to Moroccan Lamb (see page 228).

Serves: **4**

Preparation time: 15 minutes

Cooking time: 55 minutes

2 aubergines, sliced lengthways
1 onion, sliced
4 garlic cloves, peeled and sliced
1 red pepper, quartered, cored and deseeded
1 orange pepper, quartered, cored and deseeded
4 tomatoes, halved
1 red chilli, halved and deseeded
½ teaspoon caraway seeds
½ teaspoon ground cumin
50 g/2 oz pitted black olives
1 bunch of coriander, roughly chopped
2 tablespoons olive oil
sea salt and pepper
2 griddled red chillies, to garnish (optional)

1 Heat the griddle pan. Add the aubergine slices and cook for 5 minutes on each side. Place in a mixing bowl.

2 Griddle the sliced onion for 5 minutes on each side, add to the aubergine in the bowl. Then cook the garlic slices for 2 minutes on each side and add to the bowl. Griddle the pepper quarters for 5 minutes on each side, then the tomato halves for 5 minutes on the skin side, adding them all to the bowl. Finally, griddle the chilli for 5 minutes on one side then chop finely and add to the bowl.

3 Crush the caraway seeds using a pestle and mortar. Add to the griddled vegetables with the cumin, olives, roughly chopped coriander, olive oil and seasoning. Garnish with the griddled red chillies, if using. Serve the salad at room temperature.

Chickpea Salad with Griddled Vegetables and Mint

Serves: **4**

Preparation time: 10 minutes

Cooking time: 15 minutes

4 shallots
2 garlic cloves, peeled and sliced
4 large red Spanish chillies, halved lengthways
  and deseeded
300 g/10 oz can chickpeas, rinsed and drained
1 bunch of mint, roughly chopped
3 tablespoons olive oil
4 tablespoons lemon juice
sea salt and pepper

1 Heat the griddle pan. Cut the shallots into wedges, keeping the root ends intact to hold the wedges together. Cook on the griddle for 4 minutes on each side. Remove from the griddle pan and place in a large bowl.

2 Cook the garlic on the griddle for 1 minute on each side, then remove and add to the bowl containing the shallots. Griddle the Spanish chillies for a total of 5 minutes then add to the bowl.

3 Add the drained chickpeas, chopped mint, olive oil, lemon juice and seasoning to the bowl of griddled vegetables. Mix all the ingredients together roughly and serve.

Griddled Pepper and Asparagus Salad

Serves: **4**

Preparation time: 10 minutes

Cooking time: 20 minutes

4 red peppers, quartered, cored and deseeded
2 red chillies, deseeded and cut into very
  thin strips
200 g/7 oz asparagus, trimmed
4 tablespoons olive oil
1 tablespoon balsamic vinegar
75 g/3 oz Parmesan cheese
sea salt and pepper

1 Heat the griddle pan. Cook the pepper
quarters on the griddle for 5 minutes on each
side, then remove and set aside. Cook the thin
strips of chilli on the griddle, turning
frequently, for a total of 3 minutes. Remove
and set aside. Finally, griddle the asparagus
for 5 minutes, turning frequently.

2 Arrange the vegetables on a serving plate.
Drizzle with the oil and balsamic vinegar and
sprinkle with salt and pepper. Finally, using a
vegetable peeler, peel thin ribbons of
Parmesan over the vegetables. Serve with
griddled bread or serve as a side dish to
accompany griddled fish or poultry.

Couscous and Griddled Vegetable Salad

Serves: **4**

Preparation time: 15 minutes

Cooking time: 45 minutes

1 aubergine, sliced
2 garlic cloves, peeled and sliced
2 green chillies
1 red pepper
2 red onions
1 courgette, sliced
125 g/4 oz couscous
½ teaspoon cumin
½ teaspoon paprika
pinch of dried chilli flakes
5 tablespoons olive oil
sea salt and pepper
1 bunch of coriander, chopped, to garnish
1 lemon, griddled and cut into wedges, to serve
 (optional)

1 Heat the griddle pan. Place the aubergine slices on the griddle and cook for 5 minutes on each side. Remove from the pan and set aside in a large bowl. Cook the slices of garlic on the griddle for 1 minute on each side, then add to the griddled aubergine in the bowl.

2 Cook the chillies and the pepper whole – the chillies for 5 minutes and the pepper for 10 minutes – until they are charred on all sides. Set aside.

3 Meanwhile, cut the red onions into wedges, keeping the root ends intact to hold the wedges together. Griddle for 5 minutes on each side, before adding to the aubergine. Lastly, cook the courgette slices for 4 minutes on each side.

4 Place the couscous in a bowl and add enough water to cover. Leave for 5 minutes to allow all the water to be absorbed.

5 Peel the griddled chillies and pepper when cool enough to handle and chop and deseed them. Roughly chop all the griddled vegetables and add them to the bowl of couscous. Add the cumin, paprika, chilli flakes and seasoning, and mix well. Drizzle with the olive oil and garnish with the chopped coriander. Serve with the lemon wedges, if using.

FOOD FACT • Couscous is made from grains of hard durum wheat semolina and can be considered the national grain of North Africa. It is now widely available and, since it has a natural affinity with most ingredients, is a good alternative to rice. Unlike traditional couscous, the modern version is precooked and simply needs moistening, as above, and reheating if necessary.

Griddled Mushroom Salad

Serves: **4**

Preparation time: 10 minutes

Cooking time: 15–20 minutes

150 g/5 oz flat mushrooms
2 shallots
300 g/10 oz pappardelle
4 tablespoons olive oil
1 tablespoon chopped chives
sea salt and pepper

1 Heat the griddle pan. Place the mushrooms on the griddle and cook for 6 minutes. Then turn the mushrooms over and cook for another 6 minutes. Remove and set aside.

2 Cut the shallots into wedges, keeping the root ends intact to hold the wedges together. Griddle for 3 minutes on each side.

3 Meanwhile, bring a large saucepan of lightly salted water to the boil. When boiling, plunge the pasta into the water and cook for 12 minutes, or according to packet instructions.

4 Drain the cooked pasta well. Tip into a large bowl and toss in the olive oil and a little seasoning. Slice the griddled mushrooms, add to the pasta with the griddled shallots and the chives. Serve immediately or leave to cool a little and serve at room temperature.

FOOD FACT • Made with eggs and semolina, pappardelle is pasta in the form of long, wide ribbons, sometimes with a crimped edge. It has a luxurious feel when served with creamy sauces but is just as good with a simpler dressing like this one.

The Griddle Pan

Good-quality griddle pans are widely available and more and more people are discovering the benefits and pleasures of this versatile method of cooking.

The griddle pan looks like a frying pan but has distinctive ridges across the cooking surface. The pans are significantly heavier than normal frying pans because they have to withstand very high temperatures. There is a wide choice of griddle pans. They come in different sizes and may be round, oblong or square in shape. Some pans have a spout on the side for pouring off juices. Extra large griddle pans are also available, which go across two rings on the stove.

Some models have a removable handle so that the pan can be transferred to the oven to continue cooking after the food has been sealed. Others are divided by a big ridge across the pan, which separates the pan into two halves comprising a griddling surface and a flat surface for normal frying. This means that you could, for example, griddle bacon and sausages in one side of the pan while frying an egg in the other at the same time.

Buy the heaviest and best-quality griddle pan you can afford. The advantages of non-stick pans are obvious when it comes to cleaning them, but they may deteriorate before other pans. The benefit of a cast-iron griddle pan is that once heated, it retains its heat and cooks food at a steady consistent heat, emulating the kind of heat effect you get on a charcoal barbecue. It is therefore excellent for searing and griddling.

The basic method for griddling is to preheat the griddle pan so that the surface is very hot before starting to cook. The food placed on the griddle is then quickly seared on both sides to form a crust that will seal in the juices and lock in the natural flavour of the food. The crust must form before the food is turned over to sear the other side, otherwise it will stick to the pan and fall apart. Initially, the food will stick to the pan but as it cooks and seals it will lift slightly from the surface and you will be able to turn it fairly easily.

Caring for your pan

Read the manufacturer's instructions on how to care for your griddle pan. If you take good care of your pan it will give you many years of service. Good-quality non-stick pans are very easy to clean after use. Simply wash them in warm soapy water and dry thoroughly. Be especially careful not to use harsh scourers or abrasive cleaning materials, which would damage the non-stick surface. Instead use a soft cloth or sponge.

Cast-ironware requires minimum care, but generally you should not use detergents or scouring agents on cast-ironware pans. Use only hot water and a brush for cleaning, then wipe the surface thoroughly dry.

Never run water on a very hot griddle pan since this could cause the pan to warp. Similarly, never set a hot griddle pan on a cold surface as this may have the same effect.

Other useful utensils

Use utensils with your griddle pan that will preserve and protect your griddle's surface. Preferred utensils are made of nylon or wood since they will not scratch the surface of the griddle. Spatulas and tongs are the handiest tools: lightweight non-stick spatulas are ideal for turning delicate items such as fish, as are scissor-action tongs with non-stick tapered ends. Tongs are particularly good for turning and moving pieces of meat and sausages.

A palette knife is useful for turning foods, too. The long, thin, flexible blade slides under most chops and fish fillets completely so that the food won't tear or stick when it is flipped over. Take care to avoid scratching the pan when using a metal palette knife.

Griddled Fennel and Butter Bean Salad

Serves: **4**

Preparation time: 10 minutes

Cooking time: 15 minutes

2 fennel heads
2 green peppers, quartered, cored and
  deseeded
250 g/8 oz can butter beans, rinsed and drained
100 g/3½ oz feta cheese
40 g/1½ oz pine nuts, toasted (see page 40)
1 bunch parsley, chopped, plus extra to garnish
5 tablespoons olive oil
sea salt and pepper

1 Heat the griddle pan. Thinly slice the fennel lengthways, removing the hard core. Place the fennel lengths on the griddle and cook for 4–5 minutes on each side. When cooked, set aside in a bowl and keep warm.

2 Cook the pepper quarters on the griddle for 5 minutes and add to the fennel.

3 Add the well-drained butter beans to the bowl of griddled vegetables. Crumble in the feta and add the toasted pine nuts, chopped parsley, olive oil and a little seasoning. Toss and serve, garnished with more parsley.

Parma Ham and Vegetable Salad

Serves: **4**

Preparation time: 10 minutes

Cooking time: 40–45 minutes

2 red onions
2 red peppers, cored, deseeded and cut into
  flat pieces
2 courgettes, cut into long lengths
1 aubergine, cut into long lengths
1 bunch of asparagus, trimmed
8 slices of Parma ham
1 bunch of basil, roughly chopped
4 tablespoons olive oil
2 tablespoons balsamic vinegar
sea salt and pepper
basil sprig, to garnish

1 Heat the griddle pan. Cut the red onions into wedges, keeping the root ends intact to hold the wedges together. Griddle all the vegetables as follows, removing them when cooked to a large serving bowl: onions 5 minutes on each side; red peppers 5 minutes on the skin side only; courgettes 3 minutes on each side; aubergines 4 minutes on each side, and the asparagus for 4 minutes on one side only. When all the vegetables have been griddled, toss them together well in the bowl.

2 Place the slices of Parma ham on the griddle to cook for 4 minutes on each side, or until crispy.

3 Add the roughly chopped basil to the vegetables with the olive oil, balsamic vinegar and a little seasoning. Top the vegetables with the crispy Parma ham and serve immediately, garnished with a sprig of basil.

FOOD FACT • Asparagus is the young shoot of a plant, of which there are many species. It is something of a luxury because it has such a short season, available fresh in spring and early summer only. To prepare asparagus, wash it well then trim the end of each stalk by cutting across at a sharp angle just where the bright green starts to fade to a dull green colour. Peel the ends of any thick stems.

Starters & Vegetables

Griddled Vegetable Soup

This is a delicious and healthy soup, full of the flavour of fresh vegetables. Turn it into a more filling meal by adding cooked butter beans to the soup after blending.

Serves: **4**

Preparation time: 15 minutes

Cooking time: 35–40 minutes

1 red onion, sliced
4 red peppers, cored, deseeded and cut into flat pieces
2 courgettes, sliced
1 aubergine, sliced
2 garlic cloves, peeled and sliced
400 ml/14 fl oz organic tomato juice
75 g/3 oz Parmesan cheese, grated
1 bunch of basil, chopped
6 tablespoons olive oil
sea salt and pepper
bread, to serve

1 Heat the griddle pan. Begin by griddling all the vegetables as detailed below, setting them aside each time when cooked. Griddle the onion slices for 5 minutes on each side. Griddle the flat pepper pieces for 6 minutes on the skin side only, until charred and blistered. Peel when cool enough to handle.

2 Meanwhile, griddle the slices of courgette for 4 minutes on each side, the slices of aubergine for 5 minutes on each side, and the garlic slices for 1 minute on each side.

3 Place all the griddled vegetables in a blender, reserving a few slices of courgette, add the tomato juice and process roughly for a soup with a little texture or process until smooth, according to your preference.

4 Place the grated Parmesan in a small bowl. Add the chopped basil, the olive oil and a little seasoning, and mix well.

5 Check the soup and add salt and pepper to taste. Serve it hot or cold, accompanied by bread, and garnished with the reserved courgette slices and with a little of the Parmesan and basil mixture spooned in just before serving. Serve the remainder separately at the table for guests to help themselves.

Griddled Courgettes with Lemon Pesto

This makes a great dish on its own or it goes fantastically well with griddled fish such as swordfish.

Serves: **4**

Preparation time: 10 minutes

Cooking time: 12 minutes

200 g/7 oz baby courgettes
lemon zest, to garnish (optional)
lemon wedges, to serve
LEMON PESTO
1 large bunch of basil
75 g/3 oz pine nuts, toasted (see below)
2 garlic cloves, crushed
75 g/3 oz Parmesan cheese, grated
grated rind and juice of 2 lemons
4 tablespoons olive oil
sea salt and pepper

1 Heat the griddle pan. Slice the baby courgettes in half lengthways, place a batch on the griddle and cook for 3 minutes on each side. Remove and keep warm while you griddle the remaining courgettes.

2 Meanwhile, make the lemon pesto. Place the basil, toasted pine nuts, garlic, Parmesan, lemon rind and juice, olive oil and seasoning in a blender and process until smooth. Alternatively, pound the basil and pine nuts together in a mortar and pestle to form a paste, add the garlic and Parmesan and pound again, then add the remaining ingredients and mix until smooth.

3 Arrange the griddled courgettes on a serving plate or 4 individual plates. Drizzle the lemon pesto over the top and serve garnished with lemon zest, if liked, and accompanied by lemon wedges, for squeezing.

FOOD FACT • Pine nuts are the seeds from the glossy cones of pine trees. They have a creamy texture and may be eaten raw or toasted. Pine nuts are widely used in Mediterranean cooking and are an essential ingredient in pesto sauce. Keep them refrigerated but do not store them for too long since their resinous oil spoils easily and turns rancid. Toasting pine nuts brings out their nutty flavour. Spread them out on a baking sheet and place in a hot oven or under a preheated grill for a few minutes. Keep checking and shaking the baking sheet so that the pine nuts cook evenly. Watch them carefully as they are quick to burn and will then taste bitter.

Griddled Herb Fritters with Yogurt Dip

These fritters make great nibbling food. The mix can be made in advance but try and cook the fritters just before serving to retain the flavours of the fresh chopped herbs.

Serves: **4**

Preparation time: 15 minutes

Cooking time: 20 minutes

150 g/5 oz mozzarella cheese, finely chopped
1 bunch of basil, chopped
1 bunch of flat-leaf parsley, chopped
1 bunch of chives, chopped
1 garlic clove, finely chopped
100 g/3½ oz cooked mashed potato
1 egg, beaten
sea salt and pepper
chives, to garnish
YOGURT DIP
200 g/7 oz Greek yogurt
1 shallot, finely chopped
1 bunch of mint, finely chopped
1 garlic clove, finely chopped

1 Place the chopped mozzarella in a mixing bowl. Add the chopped herbs and mix well. Add the finely chopped garlic, cooked mashed potato and beaten egg. Season and mix together well.

2 Divide the mixture into 12. Shape into balls and flatten each slightly. Heat the griddle pan.

3 Place the balls of mixture on the griddle and cook the fritters in batches for 4–5 minutes on each side. Keep the griddled fritters warm until they are all cooked.

4 To make the dip, place the Greek yogurt, finely chopped shallot, mint and garlic in a bowl. Mix well and serve with the fritters. Garnish the fritters with chives.

Griddled Chicory with Parmesan

Serves: **4**

Preparation time: 5 minutes

Cooking time: 25 minutes

4 chicory heads
100 g/3½ oz Parmesan cheese, grated
sea salt and pepper
salad leaves, to serve

1 Heat the griddle pan. Slice the chicory heads in half lengthways and place them on the griddle. Cook for 5 minutes on each side. Repeat until all the chicory is cooked.

2 Place the griddled chicory in an ovenproof dish, season with salt and pepper and sprinkle with the grated Parmesan. Place the dish under a preheated grill until the Parmesan is just bubbling. Serve immediately, accompanied by salad leaves.

FOOD FACT • Chicory is a compact, spear-shaped vegetable with crisp white leaves and a slightly bitter taste. When buying chicory heads, avoid any that are showing too much green, which indicates bitterness. To prepare chicory, trim off the root base and remove any damaged outer leaves. It can be used whole, halved lengthways or sliced.

Pumpkin with Truffle Oil

Serves: **4**

Preparation time: 5 minutes

Cooking time: 40 minutes

1 kg/2 lb pumpkin or butternut squash
75 g/3 oz Parmesan cheese
4 teaspoons truffle oil
sea salt and pepper
chopped flat-leaf parsley, to garnish

1 Heat the griddle pan. Cut the pumpkin in half and remove all the seeds. Cut the flesh into 3 cm/1¼ inch wedges or slices. Peel off the skin.

2 Place some pieces of pumpkin on the griddle and cook for 10 minutes on each side. When soft, transfer the pumpkin to a plate and keep warm while you cook the remaining pumpkin in the same way.

3 Shave the Parmesan over the pumpkin using a vegetable peeler. Drizzle with the truffle oil, season well with salt and pepper and sprinkle with the chopped parsley.

FOOD FACT • Truffle oil is an olive oil that has been infused with truffles – the most prized fungi in the world, much loved for their delicious nutty texture and earthy aroma. A luxury ingredient, truffle oil is used sparingly because of its cost as well as its pungent nature – 1 teaspoon per person is sufficient. It is used mostly for dressing pasta and salads and is available from good delicatessens.

Griddled Peppers and Vegetables with Mozzarella

These stuffed griddled peppers constitute a dish of truly Mediterranean flavours. Serve with ciabatta or country bread for extra authenticity.

Serves: **4**

Preparation time: 10 minutes

Cooking time: 45 minutes

2 large red peppers, halved, cored and deseeded
2 red onions
1 small aubergine, sliced
2 garlic cloves, peeled and halved
2 courgettes, sliced
100 g/3½ oz green olives stuffed with anchovies
150 g/5 oz mozzarella, sliced
olive oil, for drizzling
sea salt and pepper

1 Heat the griddle pan. Place the pepper halves on the griddle and cook for 7 minutes on each side. Remove and set aside.

2 Cut the red onions into wedges, keeping the root ends intact to hold the wedges together. Place the onion wedges on the griddle and cook for 5 minutes on each side. Remove and set aside.

3 Rub the aubergine slices with the garlic and griddle for 5 minutes on each side, before removing from the pan and setting aside. Slice and add the garlic to the pan, if liked. Lastly, griddle the courgette slices for 5 minutes on each side.

4 Arrange the griddled vegetables in the pepper halves, together with the stuffed olives and sliced mozzarella. Season with salt and pepper, drizzle with a little olive oil and serve hot or at room temperature.

Sweetcorn and Bacon Fritters

Serves: **4**

Preparation time: 10 minutes

Cooking time: 20 minutes

300 g/10 oz canned or frozen sweetcorn
200 g/7 oz cooked, diced bacon
1 onion, finely chopped
1 bunch of sage, chopped
2 eggs, beaten
4 tablespoons cornflour
sea salt and pepper
Spicy Salsa, to serve (see page 74)

1 Place the sweetcorn and bacon in a mixing bowl. Add the finely chopped onion and the chopped sage to the bowl, then the beaten eggs, cornflour and seasoning. Mix well until the mixture is evenly blended.

2 Heat the griddle pan. When hot, place tablespoonfuls of the mixture on the griddle and cook for 3–4 minutes. The undersides of the fritters should be golden and firm when you come to turn them over carefully; cook the other side for another 3–4 minutes. Remove from the griddle and keep warm while you cook the remaining fritters. Serve with the spicy tomato salsa.

Spicy Courgette Fritters

These fritters are great served plain as an unusual side dish. An alternative, however, is to make them into a sensational starter by layering them with soured cream and smoked salmon.

Serves: **4**

Preparation time: 10 minutes

Cooking time: 20 minutes

500 g/1 lb courgettes, grated
2½ tablespoons plain flour
1 egg, beaten
1 chilli, deseeded and chopped
1 garlic clove, crushed
75 g/3 oz Cheddar cheese, grated
sea salt and pepper
TO SERVE
250 g/8 oz smoked salmon
150 ml/¼ pint soured cream
salmon eggs
griddled lemon wedges
dill sprigs

1 Place the grated courgettes on a clean tea towel, gather up the corners and twist into a tight ball to extract all excess moisture from the courgette. This is important otherwise the fritters will be soggy.

2 Mix together the flour and egg in a bowl until smooth. Add the courgette and the remaining ingredients, season and mix well.

3 Heat the griddle pan. Divide the mixture into 8 and place 4 portions of fritter mixture on the griddle. Flatten with a palette knife and cook for 4–5 minutes, then turn and cook for a further 4–5 minutes. Do not disturb the fritters while they are cooking as a crust needs to form on the cooking side, or they will be difficult to turn.

4 Keep the griddled fritters warm while you cook the remainder, until all the mixture is used. Layer the fritters with smoked salmon and soured cream and top with salmon eggs and dill. Serve with griddled lemon wedges.

Griddled Greens

Serves: **4**

Preparation time: 10 minutes

Cooking time: 20 minutes

2 courgettes, cut into battens
250 g/8 oz asparagus, trimmed
250 g/8 oz baby leeks, trimmed
2 red peppers, quartered, cored and deseeded
4 tablespoons olive oil
2 tablespoons balsamic vinegar
basil leaves, to garnish
sea salt and pepper

1 Heat the griddle pan. Place the courgettes on the griddle and cook for 6 minutes, turning occasionally. Remove from the griddle and place in a bowl.

2 Cook the prepared asparagus and leeks for 5 minutes, turning them occasionally. Remove from the griddle and add to the bowl containing the courgettes.

3 Finally, griddle the pepper pieces on one side for 5 minutes and add to the bowl. Mix the vegetables together. Add the olive oil, balsamic vinegar and seasoning to the griddled vegetables, toss and serve garnished with the basil leaves.

Griddled Potatoes with Wasabi Dipping Sauce

These potatoes are delicious served either with drinks before a meal or as a side dish with griddled trout.

Serves: **4**

Preparation time: 20 minutes

Cooking time: 40 minutes

750 g/1½ lb new potatoes
5 tablespoons mayonnaise
3 tablespoons water
wasabi paste, to taste
sea salt

1 Heat the griddle pan. Cut the potatoes in half lengthways, place on the griddle and cook for 10 minutes on each side. Check that they are almost soft then remove from the griddle, place in a dish and allow the potatoes to stand for 10 minutes to steam in their skins. Sprinkle with sea salt.

2 Blend together the mayonnaise, water and a little wasabi paste in a small bowl and serve with the potatoes.

FOOD FACT • Wasabi, or Japanese green horseradish, is unrelated to our horseradish, although it is a member of the cabbage family. Powdered wasabi, available from Japanese supermarkets, is mixed with water in the same way as English mustard powder to make a stiff paste, which is used in small quantities since it has a powerful flavour and a delayed hot taste. Alternatively, you can buy wasabi paste in tubes. Japanese cooks use wasabi in sushi.

Griddled Fennel and Onions

Serves: **4**

Preparation time: 10 minutes

Cooking time: 25 minutes

2 red onions
2 fennel heads
2 teaspoons Dijon mustard
4 tablespoons lemon juice
5 tablespoons olive oil
sea salt and pepper
TO GARNISH
lemon rind strips
chopped basil

1 Heat the griddle pan. Cut the red onions into wedges, keeping the root ends intact to hold the wedges together. Cook on the griddle for 6 minutes on each side. Set aside.

2 Cut the fennel into quarters and remove the hard core. Slice roughly, place on the griddle and cook for 6 minutes on each side.

3 Mix together the mustard and lemon juice in a small bowl. Add the olive oil and mix well.

4 Place the griddled fennel and onions in a serving dish, season and pour over the vinaigrette dressing. Garnish with lemon rind and chopped basil.

Emmental Potato Fritters

These are really delicious and very moreish. Serve as a side dish, or top with griddled bacon and serve as a tasty starter.

Serves: **4**

Preparation time: 10 minutes

Cooking time: 30 minutes

500 g/1 lb potatoes, peeled and grated
2 tablespoons plain flour
1 egg, beaten
1 onion, chopped
1 garlic clove, crushed
100 g/3½ oz Emmental cheese, grated
sea salt and pepper
TO GARNISH
basil leaves
snipped chives
TO SERVE
griddled bacon
torn radicchio leaves

1 Place the grated potato on a clean tea towel, gather up the corners and twist into a tight ball to extract all excess moisture from the potato. This is important otherwise the fritters will be soggy.

2 Mix together the flour and egg in a bowl until smooth. Add the potato and the remaining ingredients, season and mix well.

3 Heat the griddle pan. Divide the mixture into 8 and place 4 portions of fritter mixture on the griddle. Flatten with a palette knife and cook for 4–5 minutes, then turn and cook for a further 4–5 minutes. Do not disturb the fritters while they are cooking as a crust needs to form on the cooking side, or they will be difficult to turn.

4 Keep the griddled fritters warm while you cook the remainder until all the mixture is used. Garnish with basil and snipped chives. Serve as an unusual side dish or with griddled bacon and radicchio as a starter.

Vegetables & Cheese

The simple rule that the fresher the vegetable, the more simply it should be cooked, is never more true than for griddling. The best flavour comes from natural ingredients either grown organically or gathered from the wild. Organically-grown vegetables are produced without the use of chemical fertilizers or pesticides. Because they are grown naturally they tend to contain less water and therefore often have a more concentrated flavour, as well as higher nutrient levels. Organic produce is now widely available and is certainly worth trying if you have not already done so.

Vegetables

Vegetables are certainly the easiest ingredients to griddle, although not all vegetables are suited to this method of cooking. The best are aubergines, courgettes, fennel, onions, peppers, mushrooms, asparagus and mangetout. Thin slices of carrot and parsnip are tasty, too; other possibilities are new and sweet potatoes, leeks, beetroot and pumpkin. As with other foods, griddling vegetables gives them the look and taste of food cooked over an outdoor barbecue, with the characteristic scorch marks and the smoky flavour.

The usual basic principles of griddling apply: the idea is not to burn the vegetables but to brown them. If the vegetables do not move easily when you try to turn them, leave them a little longer. They should cook briskly as if they were being fried.

Vegetables don't require any special preparation before griddling. However, pick your ingredients with care and don't use any that are past their best. For example, choose firm tomatoes – even those that are slightly green are ideal for griddling since they are less juicy and hold their shape better when griddled than fully ripe ones.

The way vegetables are cut affects their appearance, taste and cooking qualities. Once cut, all vegetables begin to dry up and lose nutrients through oxidation by exposure to air, so it is always best, if possible, to cut them just before you need them. If you want to griddle wedges of onions, rather than slices, you will need to keep their root ends intact, otherwise they will fall apart on the griddle.

Most vegetables can be griddled just as they are, but a rubdown with garlic or lemon juice first can give them a bit of a zip. Once griddled, you can serve them plain or, even better, with some type of sauce, for example aïoli, which is a garlic mayonnaise (see page 64), or a pesto (see page 10), or top them with knobs of savoury butter which melt over the hot vegetables and impart a delicious spicy or herby flavour (see page 11).

Vegetables can also be griddled in the form of kebabs. Cut them into chunks of an even size

and thread them on to presoaked wooden skewers. The thing to remember when combining vegetables with meat or fish on skewers, is that you need to select foods that will cook in the same amount of time. For example, prawns cook quickly so pick vegetables such as mushrooms and cherry tomatoes. Team cubes of meat, which take a little longer to cook, with pieces of pepper, onion or courgette which take just as long.

Cheese

Certain cheeses can be cooked successfully on the griddle. Firm ripe goats' and sheep's cheeses are most suitable and the best-known are the Greek feta cheese (see page 82) and haloumi (see page 222), which originally came from Cyprus. If you feel adventurous, experiment with any cheese with similar characteristics to either of these; ask in a cheese shop or at the delicatessen counter of a supermarket for suggestions.

To griddle haloumi, remove it from its plastic wrapping and pat it dry with kitchen paper. Cut the cheese into thick slices and place on a hot griddle for a few minutes to crisp the outside while the inside melts. Remove the cheese from the griddle and serve it, drizzled with a little flavoured oil (see page 118) and accompanied by a crisp green salad and chunks of country bread. This makes an ideal lunch or supper dish, and is especially popular with vegetarians.

Griddled Vegetables with Aïoli

Serves: **4**

Preparation time: 10 minutes

Cooking time: 20–30 minutes

selection of seasonal vegetables for griddling,
    such as asparagus, peppers, red onion, fennel,
    aubergine, potatoes, baby leeks
    and courgettes
chopped parsley, to garnish
AIOLI
2 egg yolks
½ teaspoon Dijon mustard
2 garlic cloves, crushed
2 tablespoons lemon juice
175 ml/6 fl oz olive oil
sea salt and pepper

1 Prepare the vegetables by cutting into chunks or wedges. Preheat the griddle pan before you begin. Griddle your chosen vegetables as follows, remove from the pan when cooked and set aside. Griddle trimmed asparagus stalks for 4 minutes, turning them frequently. Griddle pepper quarters for 5 minutes on one side and red onion wedges for 4 minutes on each side. Griddle fennel and aubergine slices for 5 minutes on each side. Griddle thin slices of potato for 10 minutes on each side, baby leeks for 5 minutes and slices of courgette for 4 minutes on each side.

2 To make the aïoli, place the egg yolks, Dijon mustard, garlic and lemon juice in a blender and process. With the motor running, very slowly drizzle in the olive oil – a few drops to begin with and then in a thin stream. Process until the mixture is thick. Season the aïoli to taste then serve with the griddled vegetables, garnished with chopped parsley.

Aubergine Wraps

Serves: **4**

Preparation time: 8 minutes

Cooking time: 20 minutes

1 large aubergine
2 red onions, thinly sliced
125 g/4 oz Gruyère cheese, thinly sliced
2 beefsteak tomatoes, skinned and sliced
olive oil, for drizzling
sea salt and pepper
chopped chives, to garnish
radicchio salad, to serve

1 Heat the griddle pan. Cut the aubergine lengthways into thin slices, place on the griddle and cook for 5 minutes on each side. Remove and set aside.

2 Place the red onion slices on the griddle and cook for 4 minutes on each side.

3 To assemble the wraps, take the 4 best slices of aubergine and lay them on a plate. Towards one end of each aubergine slice place slices of Gruyère, red onion and tomato. Season and fold the other end of the aubergine over the top.

4 Garnish with the chopped chives and serve with a radicchio salad and the extra aubergine slices, drizzled with olive oil and seasoned.

FOOD FACT • Aubergines come in a wide range of colours, shapes and sizes. The dark purple-skinned aubergines are probably the most familiar. These modern commercial aubergines are not as bitter as the traditional varieties, and so do not necessitate salting before use to draw out the bitter juices. Choose aubergines with bright, glossy skins, avoiding any that are dull or wrinkled. There is no difference in flavour between large and baby aubergines. Store aubergines in a cool place, not the fridge, and they will stay in good condition for up to 2 weeks.

Fish

Griddled Salmon with Soured Cream and Fish Eggs

This recipe is so simple to make but very tasty, especially when served with parsley mashed potatoes.

Serves: **4**

Preparation time: 5 minutes

Cooking time: 8–10 minutes

4 x 150 g/5 oz salmon fillets, skinned
150 ml/¼ pint soured cream
100 g/3½ oz black and/or orange fish eggs
pepper
chopped spring onions, to garnish
TO SERVE
Creamy Mashed Potatoes (see page 76)
3 tablespoon chopped parsley
griddled lemon wedges

1 Heat the griddle pan. Place the salmon fillets on the griddle and cook for 4–5 minutes on each side.

2 When cooked, arrange the fish on 4 individual plates and spoon soured cream on top. Top with fish eggs and chopped spring onions, and season with black pepper. Serve with creamy mashed potatoes mixed with the chopped parsley and griddled lemon wedges.

FOOD FACT • Fish eggs come in a variety of sizes and colours. Those most widely available are the eggs of the lumpfish, which have been salted, coloured black or red and pressed. Most often from Denmark, Iceland and Germany, lumpfish roe is relatively inexpensive compared to caviare – roe from the sevruga, osetra and beluga fish of the sturgeon family.

Griddled Trout with Horseradish Salad

Serves: **4**

Preparation time: 10 minutes

Cooking time: 8 minutes

4 x 175 g/6 oz trout fillets, skinned
50 g/2 oz fresh horseradish
100 g/3½ red radishes
100 g/3½ oz baby spinach leaves
2 tablespoons cider vinegar
5 tablespoons olive oil, plus extra for drizzling
sea salt and pepper

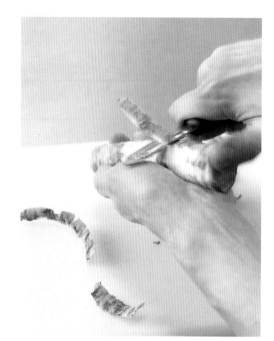

1 Heat the griddle pan. Wipe the trout fillets with kitchen paper, place on the griddle and cook for 4 minutes on each side. Do not try to turn the fillets too early or they will break.

2 Meanwhile, peel and grate the horseradish on a medium to small sized grater. Trim and cut the radishes into quarters.

3 Toss the grated horseradish in a bowl with the radishes, baby spinach, cider vinegar, olive oil and seasoning. Mix well and divide among 4 plates. Place the griddled trout on the plates. Drizzle over a little olive oil, season and serve.

FOOD FACT • Horseradish is the dirty yellowish coloured root of a plant belonging to the mustard family. It has a hot pungent taste and is best used sparingly. When buying it, choose roots that are firm and fat. Scrub the piece vigorously or peel it, then grate as much as you need of the outer part. The inner core is very tough and weaker in flavour so can be discarded. Horseradish keeps for several weeks in the salad drawer of the refrigerator, but starts to lose its pungency once grated. Any leftover grated horseradish can be frozen.

Griddled Sea Bass with Spicy Salsa

This spicy tomato salsa provides a good contrast in both flavour and texture to the smooth meaty flesh of griddled sea bass.

Serves: **4**

Preparation time: 15 minutes, plus standing

Cooking time: 6–8 minutes

4 x 175 g/6 oz sea bass fillets
SPICY SALSA
4 plum tomatoes, skinned and deseeded
1 chilli, finely chopped
2 garlic cloves, finely chopped
50 g/2 oz black olives, pitted and finely chopped
1 shallot, finely chopped
4 tablespoons olive oil
4 tablespoons lemon juice
sea salt and pepper
parsley sprigs, to garnish
TO SERVE
freshly cooked tagliatelle
spinach salad
lemon wedges

1 To make the spicy salsa, roughly chop the tomatoes and place them in a large bowl. Add the finely chopped chilli, garlic, olives and shallot, the olive oil, lemon juice and a little seasoning. Mix well and set aside, allowing the flavours to blend for at least 1 hour.

2 Heat the griddle pan. Cook the sea bass fillets for 3–4 minutes on each side, then garnish with parsley. Serve with the spicy salsa, tagliatelle, a spinach salad and lemon wedges for squeezing.

FOOD FACT • Plum tomatoes are grown in southern Europe primarily for canning but they are also available fresh. They have relatively small seed clusters and a dryer pulp than the standard round tomato. Always choose firm unblemished tomatoes with a hint of fragrance, which is a good indication of flavour. The skin can be removed from plum tomatoes fairly easily (see page 230). To deseed them cut across the tomatoes to halve them. Hold each tomato half in your hand and squeeze it gently over a bowl, shaking as you do so; the seeds will fall into the bowl and can be discarded.

Herb-crusted Pink Salmon

Serves: **4**

Preparation time: 15 minutes

Cooking time: 8–10 minutes

4 x 150 g/5 oz salmon fillets, skinned
2 shallots, finely chopped
1 large bunch of dill, roughly chopped
3 tablespoons plain flour
1 egg white
sea salt and pepper
Creamy Mashed Potatoes, to serve

1 Pat the salmon fillets dry with kitchen paper. Mix together the finely chopped shallot and the dill in a dish and season. Tip the flour on to a large plate and tip the egg white into a dish. Whisk the egg white lightly.

2 Heat the griddle pan. Dip the salmon fillets in the flour and coat them well all over. Next, dip the salmon in the egg white, again coating the fillets all over. Finally, dip the salmon in the shallot and dill mix, patting the mixture on to the fish to give it an even coating.

3 Place the salmon fillets on the griddle and cook for 4–5 minutes on each side, using a palette knife to turn the fillets over. Serve at once with creamy mashed potatoes.

Creamy Mashed Potatoes

Serves: **4**

Preparation time: 10 minutes

Cooking time: 20–25 minutes

750 g/1½ lb potatoes, such as Desirée, peeled
75 ml/3 fl oz fruity olive oil, plus extra to serve
salt and pepper

1 Boil the potatoes in salted water for 15–20 minutes until very tender. Drain and leave to steam in the colander for 5 minutes.

2 Push the potatoes through a potato ricer or mash them by hand. With an electric whisk, beat in the olive oil and continue beating for a few minutes over the heat – the mash will be nice and fluffy. Season well with salt and lots of black pepper. Serve drizzled with a little more olive oil.

Griddled Tuna, Potato and Spinach Salad

Lovage could be used in place of the spinach in this salad, if preferred. Both go equally well with the summery taste of new potatoes.

Serves: **4**

Preparation time: 10 minutes

Cooking time: 15 minutes

500 g/1 lb Jersey Royals or other small
   new potatoes
4 x 175 g/6 oz slices of tuna
100 g/3½ oz baby spinach leaves,
   roughly chopped
4 tablespoons olive oil
2 tablespoons balsamic vinegar
sea salt and pepper
griddled lime wedges, to serve

1 Clean the new potatoes but do not peel them. Place them in a steamer over boiling water and cook for 15 minutes or until soft. (Alternatively, you could boil the potatoes if you don't have a steamer.)

2 Meanwhile, heat the griddle pan. Pat the tuna fillets dry with kitchen paper and place on the griddle to cook for 3 minutes on each side for rare, 5 minutes for medium or 8 minutes for well done.

3 Remove the potatoes from the steamer. Slice them in half and place in a bowl. Add the roughly chopped spinach, olive oil and balsamic vinegar. Toss and season to taste. Divide the salad between 4 plates and serve with a slice of tuna arranged on the top of each, and a lime wedge for squeezing.

Griddled Red Snapper on Dijon-style Leaves

Serves: **4**

Preparation time: 10 minutes

Cooking time: 10 minutes

4 x 175 g/6 oz red snapper fillets
200 g/7 oz Dijon-style leaves
   (French salad leaves) or Chinese cabbage
2 teaspoons pumpkin seeds
2 teaspoons sunflower seeds
2 tablespoons olive oil
1 bunch of spring onions, shredded or
   diagonally sliced, to garnish
freshly cooked egg noodles, to serve

1 Heat the griddle pan. Pat the red snapper fillets dry with kitchen paper and cook on the griddle for 4 minutes on each side.

2 Meanwhile, toss together the salad leaves, the pumpkin and sunflower seeds and the olive oil. Arrange the dressed salad leaves on individual plates and place a red snapper fillet on top of each. Sprinkle with shredded spring onion and serve at once with noodles.

Red Mullet Wrapped Around Spinach and Feta

Serves: **4**

Preparation time: 20 minutes

Cooking time: 15 minutes

125 g/4 oz spinach, trimmed
4 x 175 g/6 oz red mullet fillets
100 g/3½ oz feta cheese, sliced into 4
1 beefsteak tomato, skinned and sliced into 4
4 marjoram sprigs, plus extra to garnish
sea salt and pepper
TO SERVE
olive oil, for drizzling
griddled lemon wedges
rocket or leafy salad

1 Place the prepared spinach in a steamer over boiling water and steam for 4 minutes. Remove the spinach and leave it until it is cool enough to handle.

2 Lay the red mullet fillets, skin side down, on a work surface. Divide the steamed spinach between the 4 fillets, placing it on top of each fillet towards one end.

3 Place the slices of feta on top of the spinach, and the tomato slices on top of the feta. Finally, add a little seasoning and a sprig of marjoram to each fillet. Fold the red mullet fillet over the top of the filling and secure with cocktail sticks.

4 Heat the griddle pan. Place the fillets on to cook for 5 minutes on each side, taking care not to break them up when turning.

5 To serve, remove the cocktail sticks. Drizzle the fish with a little olive oil and squeeze the lemon over the top. Scatter with marjoram and serve with a leafy salad.

FOOD FACT • Feta cheese is a fresh white, crumbly, salty, rindless cheese, probably best known today for its appearance in Greek salads in combination with tomato, cucumber and olives. Feta was originally made from sheep's milk but is now made from both goats' and cows' milk. Its saltiness can be reduced by soaking the cheese in cold water or milk for a few minutes before use.

Parma Ham-wrapped Salmon

Serves: **4**

Preparation time: 10 minutes

Cooking time: 10 minutes

4 x 175 g/6 oz salmon fillets, skinned
4 thin slices of fontina cheese, rind removed
16 sage leaves
8 thin slices of Parma ham
sea salt and pepper
TO SERVE
freshly cooked pasta tossed in parsley
rocket leaves
1 tablespoon olive oil
1 tablespoon balsamic vinegar

1 Season the salmon fillets and trim the slices of fontina to fit on top of the salmon.

2 Place a slice of the trimmed cheese on top of each salmon fillet, followed by 4 sage leaves. Then wrap 2 pieces of Parma ham around each salmon fillet to hold the cheese and bay leaves in place.

3 Heat the griddle pan. Cook the wrapped salmon fillets for 5 minutes on each side, taking care when turning them over. Serve with freshly cooked pasta tossed in parsley and a rocket salad dressed with balsamic vinegar and olive oil.

Sesame Tuna with Dipping Sauce

Serves: **4**

Preparation time: 10 minutes

Cooking time: 6–16 minutes

575 g/1 lb 3 oz tuna fillet or 2 fillets weighing
   about 300 g/10 oz each, skinned
3 tablespoons black sesame seeds
3 tablespoons white sesame seeds, toasted
1 egg white
sea salt
cooked spinach, to serve
DIPPING SAUCE
100 ml/3½ fl oz soy sauce
1 chilli, finely chopped
1 garlic clove, crushed

1 Pat the tuna fillet dry with kitchen paper. Mix together the sesame seeds and pour on to a plate. Tip the egg white into a dish and whisk lightly.

2 Dip the tuna in the egg white to coat it all over then dip it in the sesame seeds and pat them on to the tuna to coat the fish thoroughly with the seeds.

3 Heat the griddle pan. Slice the tuna diagonally and place the slices on the hot griddle and cook for 3 minutes on each side for rare, 5 minutes for medium or 8 minutes for well done.

4 To make the dipping sauce, combine the soy sauce, finely chopped chilli and the crushed garlic and pour into 4 little dishes. Season the tuna slices with salt, then serve on individual plates with cooked spinach and with the sauce served separately.

FOOD FACT • Sesame seeds have a rich, sweet, slightly burnt flavour, which is enhanced by toasting, or dry-frying them before use until they jump vigorously in the pan. Black sesame seeds are less common than white ones but taste the same; the choice of black sesame seeds is therefore more often for the sake of appearance.

Sardines Stuffed with Lemon

Sardines are absolutely delicious when griddled. Lemons have always had a natural affinity with this tasty oily little fish.

Serves: **3 (or 4 as an appetizer)**

Preparation time: 10–14 minutes

Cooking time: 10 minutes

12 sardines, gutted
2 lemons, cut into thin wedges
4 plum tomatoes, skinned and diced
1 red onion, sliced
3 tablespoons olive oil
sea salt and black pepper
2 tablespoons chopped flat-leaf parsley,
  to garnish

1 Rinse the sardines in cold water. Pat dry with kitchen paper.

2 Heat the griddle pan. Stuff the stomach cavity of each sardine with a lemon wedge and secure with a cocktail stick. Place on the griddle and cook for 5–7 minutes on each side. Take care when turning the sardines as they are fragile.

3 Arrange the tomato and red onion attractively on a serving plate, drizzle with the olive oil and sprinkle with salt and pepper.

4 When the sardines are cooked, remove the cocktail sticks and serve them on the tomato and onion salad, garnished with parsley. Serve as an appetizer with a chilled glass of sherry.

Griddled Trout Fillets with Ginger and Lime Drizzle

A colourful vegetable stir-fry with courgettes, leeks, red pepper and sesame seeds makes a healthy and delicious accompaniment to this dish.

Serves: **4**

Preparation time: 10 minutes

Cooking time: 8 minutes

4 x 175 g/6 oz trout fillets
4 cm/1½ inch piece of fresh root ginger,
  peeled and finely chopped
1 chilli, finely chopped
1 garlic clove, crushed
grated rind and juice of 3 limes
coriander sprig, to garnish
TO SERVE
250 g /8 oz cooked rice noodles
stir-fried mixed vegetables (optional)

1 Heat the griddle pan. Fold the trout fillets in half lengthways, skin side out and secure with cocktail sticks. Place on the griddle and cook for 4 minutes on each side.

2 Mix together the finely chopped ginger, the chilli and garlic and the lime rind and juice in a small bowl.

3 Remove the cocktail sticks. Serve the trout fillets on a bed of rice noodles with the lime drizzle poured over the top and garnished with coriander. Accompany with a mixed vegetable stir-fry, if liked.

FOOD FACT • Fresh root ginger dries out quickly so is best bought in small quantities. Buy a root that is fat and smooth, which will be juicy, as opposed to dry and shrivelled, which will be tough. Store it in the salad drawer of the refrigerator to keep it fresh, where it should keep for 3–4 weeks. Peel the root using a vegetable peeler. Instead of chopping it, you could grate it using a fine grater.

Griddled Sea Bass with Tarragon Pesto

Griddling is a superb way of cooking this supreme firm, white-fleshed fish, which is well suited to strong flavours, such as this pesto.

Serves: **4**

Preparation time: 10 minutes

Cooking time: 8 minutes

4 x 175 g/6 oz sea bass fillets
tarragon sprig, to garnish
TARRAGON PESTO
1 bunch of tarragon
1 bunch of flat leaf parsley
1 shallot, chopped
1 garlic clove, crushed
50 g/2 oz walnuts
50 g/2 oz pine nuts, toasted (see page 40)
5 tablespoons olive oil
TO SERVE
new potatoes, steamed or boiled
tomato wedges
purple basil

1 Heat the griddle pan. Fold the sea bass fillets in half lengthways, skin side out (or remove the skin), and secure with cocktail sticks. Place on the griddle and cook for 4 minutes on each side, taking care when turning them over.

2 To make the pesto, place the tarragon, parsley, chopped shallot, garlic, walnuts, toasted pine nuts and olive oil in a blender. Process for 10 seconds for a rough-textured pesto and slightly longer for a smooth one. Alternatively, pound all the ingredients together in a mortar and pestle.

3 Remove the cocktail sticks and serve the griddled sea bass with generous amounts of the pesto, accompanied by steamed or boiled new potatoes, tomato wedges and purple basil. Garnish with a sprig of tarragon.

Oriental Monkfish

Serves: **4**

Preparation time: 20 minutes

Cooking time: 16–20 minutes

800 g/1 lb 10 oz trimmed monkfish fillets
3 cm/1¼ inch piece of fresh root ginger, peeled
  and finely chopped
3 cm/1¼ inch piece of galangal, peeled and
  finely chopped
2 garlic cloves, chopped
2 kaffir lime leaves, cut into very thin strips
1 lemon grass stalk, very finely sliced
2 red chillies, chopped
4 tablespoons lime juice
2 tablespoons soy sauce
200 g/7 oz pak choi
2 lemon grass stalks, griddled, to garnish
  (optional)
freshly boiled rice, to serve

1 Heat the griddle pan. Pat the monkfish dry with kitchen paper and place on the griddle to cook for 8–10 minutes on each side.

2 Meanwhile, mix the ginger and galangal with the chopped garlic, kaffir lime leaves, sliced lemon grass and chopped red chillies in a bowl with the lime juice and soy sauce.

3 Cut the pak choi in half or into wedges and place them in a steamer over boiling water. Steam for 3 minutes.

4 When the monkfish is cooked remove from the griddle, place on a chopping board and slice into rounds. Toss the monkfish, pak choi and oriental dressing together and serve garnished with the griddled lemon grass stalks and accompanied by boiled rice.

FOOD FACT • Pak choi is one of the best Chinese brassicas, with its broad juicy stems and mildly mustardy green leaves, which are similar in appearance to chard. It can be eaten raw in salads or stir-fried and is used extensively in Chinese cooking.

Bruschetta with Red Mullet and Olive Tapenade

Bruschetta is usually made by toasting the bread under a grill or in the oven. Here it is successfully griddled and topped with griddled fish and tapenade, perfect for a light lunch or snack. To make more of a meal of it, serve with griddled aubergine slices and skinned, chopped fresh tomatoes.

Serves: **4**

Preparation time: 10 minutes

Cooking time: 10–15 minutes

½ large French stick
4 x 175 g/6 oz red mullet fillets
1 tablespoon capers
100 g/3½ oz pitted black olives
2 garlic cloves, peeled
2 tablespoons olive oil, plus extra for drizzling
1 lemon, cut into wedges
sea salt and pepper
basil leaves, to garnish

1 Heat the griddle pan. Make the bruschetta by cutting 4 slices from the French stick, cutting the bread on the diagonal so that the slices are big enough to place the fish on. Place the bread on the griddle and cook for 3 minutes on each side. Remove from the griddle to an ovenproof dish, drizzle with olive oil and keep warm.

2 Place the fish fillets on the griddle, skin side down. Cook on one side only for 4–6 minutes, depending on the thickness of the fillets.

3 Place the capers, olives and garlic on a chopping board and chop finely. Place in a bowl and mix with the olive oil and a little salt and pepper to make a tapenade.

4 To serve, place the griddled fish on the bruschetta and top with a spoonful of the tapenade and a wedge of lemon. Garnish with basil leaves and serve warm.

Salmon Steaks with Oriental Sauce and Noodles

Serves: **4**

Preparation time: 10 minutes

Cooking time: 8 minutes

4 x 175 g/6 oz salmon steaks or fillets
4 tablespoons teriyaki sauce
4 tablespoons oyster sauce
4 tablespoons hoisin sauce
½ teaspoon Tabasco sauce
200 g/7 oz dried Chinese noodles
1 chilli, finely chopped
1 bunch of spring onions, cut into
  long thin strips
1 bunch of coriander, roughly chopped
2 tablespoons sesame oil
TO GARNISH
griddled chillies
coriander sprigs

1 Heat the griddle pan. Place the salmon fillets or steaks on the griddle and cook for 4 minutes on each side.

2 Meanwhile, mix together the teriyaki, oyster, hoisin and Tabasco sauces. Heat gently in a small bowl in the microwave or in a small saucepan on the stove.

3 Bring a large saucepan of lightly salted water to the boil. When boiling, add the noodles and cook for 3 minutes. Drain well.

4 Add the finely chopped chilli to the noodles, together with the spring onions, chopped coriander and sesame oil; toss well. Arrange the noodles and griddled salmon on individual plates, garnished with griddled chillies and corinader sprigs, with the oriental sauce served separately.

FOOD FACT • Teriyaki, oyster and hoisin sauces are all Asian in origin and widely used. Teriyaki is a mixture of soy sauce, sugar, ginger and spices, often made up as a marinade for meat and poultry but also commercially available ready-made. Oyster sauce is a thick sauce, made from oysters cooked in soy sauce and brine. It is brown in colour and both sweet and salty in taste. Hoisin is dark reddish-brown in colour and sweet and spicy tasting. It is made from soya beans, garlic, chillies and spices. Tabasco is the classic fiery hot peppery sauce from Louisiana, made from red chillies, white vinegar and salt.

Sweet Paprika Monkfish with Peppers

Serves: **4**

Preparation time: 10 minutes

Cooking time: 17 minutes

4 x 175 g/6 oz monkfish fillets
2 teaspoons Spanish paprika
4 red peppers
700 g/1 lb 7 oz small new potatoes, boiled
  or steamed
olive oil, for drizzling
sea salt and pepper
purple basil, to garnish

FOOD FACT • Paprika is a fine powder made from mild varieties of the capsicum pepper. The core and seeds are removed from the pepper then the flesh is dried and powdered. Paprika varies in taste from mildly hot to mild and sweet, and ranges in colour from rosy brown to a rich scarlet. Hungarian and Spanish are the best-known types of paprika. Spanish paprika comes in two forms – *dulce*, which is smoky, mild and sweet, and *picante*, which is hot and spicy.

1 Pat the monkfish dry with kitchen paper. Place in a dish with the paprika and coat all over with the spice. Heat the griddle pan.

2 Cut the peppers into quarters, leaving the stalks on. Remove the cores and seeds and place the pepper quarters on the griddle. Cook for 7 minutes on the skin side only, then place in a dish and keep warm.

3 Place the monkfish on the griddle and cook for 5 minutes on each side. When cooked, slice into rounds. Serve the fish with the griddled peppers and cooked new potatoes, drizzled with olive oil and sprinkled with salt and pepper to taste. Garnish with purple basil.

Spicy Crusted Swordfish

This spicy coating not only gives the swordfish an attractive appearance, but it also imparts a delicious spiciness to the firm oily flesh.

Serves: **4**

Preparation time: 10 minutes

Cooking time: 10 minutes

4 x 175 g/6 oz swordfish fillets, skinned
2 garlic cloves, crushed
1 bunch of coriander, chopped
2 teaspoons paprika
1 teaspoon ground cumin
1 teaspoon finely crushed coriander seeds
  or ground coriander
pinch of dried chilli flakes
1 onion, finely chopped
1 egg white
TO SERVE
griddled lemon wedges
griddled vegetables
Harissa (see page 226)

1 Pat the swordfish fillets dry with kitchen paper. Mix together the garlic, coriander, paprika, cumin, coriander seeds, chilli flakes and onion and spread out on a plate.

2 Tip the egg white into a dish and whisk lightly. Dip the swordfish fillets in the egg white. When well coated with egg white, dip the swordfish into the spice mixture on the plate and coat the fish all over evenly.

3 Heat the griddle pan. Place the fish on the griddle and cook for 5 minutes on each side. Serve the swordfish with lemon wedges, griddled vegetables and a little harissa.

Cod in Prosciutto with Goats' Cheese and Chives

Serves: **4**

Preparation time: 10 minutes

Cooking time: 10 minutes

4 x 175 g/6 oz cod fillets, skinned
75 g/3 oz goats' cheese, sliced
1 bunch of chives, chopped
8–12 thin slices of prosciutto or Parma ham
sea salt and pepper
whole and chopped chives, to garnish
mixed leaf salad, to serve

1 Season the cod fillets. Divide the goats' cheese between the fish, placing it on top of each fillet. Sprinkle with the chopped chives. Wrap 2–3 slices of Parma ham around each cod fillet to hold the cheese and herbs in place.

2 Heat the griddle pan. Place the prepared cod on the griddle and cook for 5 minutes on each side, taking care when turning each fillet. Garnish with the chives and serve with a mixed leaf salad.

FOOD FACT • Goats' cheeses (chèvres) are increasingly popular and there is now a wide range available. Young soft goats' cheese is a rindless fresh cheese with a mild clean flavour. Ripened firm goats' cheese has a rind and a drier texture. It is often sliced and grilled. There are many varieties of goats' cheese but they generally taste nutty and sweetish.

Shellfish

Sticky Ginger Prawns

These prawns are delicious and make an impressive dish. Serve them with Chinese rice noodles or egg noodles

Serves: **4**

Preparation time: 10 minutes

Cooking time: about 10 minutes

800 g/1 lb 10 oz large raw green prawns
   or tiger prawns, peeled and deveined
1 teaspoon vegetable oil
4 cm/1½ inch piece of fresh root ginger,
   peeled and finely chopped
2 garlic cloves, crushed
2 shallots, finely chopped
4 tablespoons brown sugar
1 tablespoon white vinegar
2 tablespoons water
2 tablespoons soy sauce
freshly cooked noodles, to serve
TO GARNISH
shredded spring onions
orange rind strips

1 Heat the griddle pan. Place the prawns on the griddle and cook for 6–8 minutes, depending on their size.

2 Meanwhile, heat the oil in a small saucepan and add the ginger, garlic and shallots. Cook for a few minutes but do not allow to brown. Add the brown sugar, white vinegar, water and soy sauce. Simmer carefully for 3–5 minutes over a low heat, and stir frequently so that the liquid evaporates away to produce a rich coating sauce.

3 Serve the prawns on a nest of noodles with the sticky sauce drizzled over the top. Garnish with shredded spring onions and orange rind.

Fish in the Pan

Fish is ideal for griddling, but it is a little trickier than griddling meat or vegetables because the flesh is more delicate and excess movement will break it apart. You should therefore avoid moving the fish on the griddle and turn it over only once. Griddling is best suited to flat whole fish, and steaks from meaty fish such as tuna and swordfish, as well as large prawns and scallops.

To tell when fish is cooked, insert the tip of a pointed knife or skewer into the thickest part of the flesh, or by the backbone if the fish is whole. If the flesh parts easily and there is no resistance, it is ready. When the fish is done, serve it immediately on warmed plates. Try to cook the fish just before you want to serve it as it will not respond well to keeping warm.

Choosing fish

A really fresh fish looks almost alive: shiny and slithery in your hands. Its colour is bright, the flesh firm and rigid yet elastic to the touch. The eyes should be bright and bulging with black pupils. Greyish pupils are a clear indication of staleness. The gills should be clean and bright red. Dark, dirty or slimy gills again indicate a bad fish. Fish should also smell fresh – an offensive odour indicates staleness.

Avoid fish that have been on sale too long and, if possible, those that have been frozen, thawed out and sold as 'fresh'. Absolute freshness is essential for oily fish, since these are inedible when stale.

Fish suitable for griddling

Wash saltwater fish in cold water to remove any bacteria and pat dry with kitchen paper; freshwater fish is more fragile and should simply be wiped clean.

For marinating fish, choose an oil-based marinade for white fish to moisten and add flavour. For oily fish, use an acidic marinade (see page 8) based on citrus juice or vinegar to offset its richness.

Cod

The flesh is succulent when fresh and keeps its texture of large firm flakes well. Fresh cod is sold mostly as steaks and fillets. If possible, choose a cut from the middle, which combines the tenderness of the tail with the flavour of the shoulder. Rubbing the flesh with lemon juice before cooking helps whiten and tenderize it.

Sardine

Fresh sardines are sold whole and vary in size, which will determine how many you need per person. To prepare sardines, cut the head almost through from the backbone and pull. As the head comes off the gut will come with it.

Tuna

Tuna is another oily fish. Take care when cooking not to overcook it or it will be dry. It is sold fresh in steaks. Look for an even, deep reddish colour. Avoid tuna with dark marks which indicate bruising.

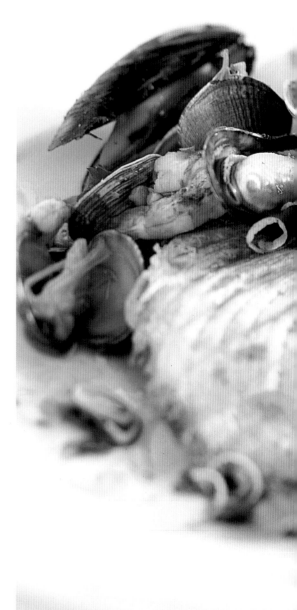

Swordfish

With its firm meaty texture and oily flesh, swordfish is perfect for griddling. It is often marinated in wine, oil and herbs before cooking. It is sold fresh in steaks.

Sea bass

Sea bass, striped or black, has a delicate flavour and a silky smooth meaty texture when griddled.

Red snapper

This weighty fish is pleasantly textured and well flavoured. It is sold fresh, whole or in steaks and fillets.

Red mullet

The flavour of red mullet is quite distinctive – something between prawn and sole. The fish is sold whole and large fish are less bony than tiny ones.

Monkfish

This ugly fish is usually sold headless. Its skin is smooth and easy to remove, as is the translucent membrane beneath, and the flesh is firm, boneless and very white. A good tail piece can be sliced or cooked whole. Monkfish has little intrinsic flavour so is best marinated or served with a rich sauce.

Salmon

Fresh salmon is sold whole or in steaks. Avoid steaks that look soft, greyish, oily or watery. Serve hot salmon with rich sauces or melted butter. Cold salmon is best with mayonnaise or with horseradish in crème fraîche.

Prawns

Fresh raw prawns are ideal for the griddle pan. When buying them, look for those that are springy to the touch, with bright crisp shells. Avoid any that are soft or limp or have a smell of ammonia about them.

Peeling raw prawns

Fresh raw prawns are usually sold with the heads already removed but the shells still intact. Before cooking, they should be peeled and their thin vein-like intestinal tracts removed. Remove the heads if not already removed. With your thumbs, split open the prawn's thin shell along the concave side, between its two rows of legs. Peel away the shell, leaving, if you like, the last segment with tail fin intact and attached to the meat. Using a small sharp knife, carefully make a shallow slit along the peeled prawn's back, just deep enough to expose the long dark vein running down its back. With the tip of the knife or your fingers, lift up and pull out the vein and discard.

Butterflying prawns

After deveining, large prawns may be butterflied to help them cook more evenly. This involves cutting them horizontally by continuing the slit down into the prawn's back, to open it out and flatten into a shape resembling a butterfly.

Griddled Bacon-wrapped Scallops

Scallops are a particular favourite among shellfish lovers. Take care not to overcook them or they will become tough.

Serves: **4**

Preparation time: 10 minutes

Cooking time: 8 minutes

12 smoked streaky bacon rashers
12 large Scottish scallops, cleaned
4 eggs or quails' eggs, soft boiled (see Notes page 4)
200 g/7 oz mixed salad leaves
4 tablespoons olive oil
4 tablespoons lemon juice
sea salt and pepper
TO GARNISH
grated lemon rind
snipped chives

1 Heat the griddle pan. Wrap a rasher of bacon around each scallop and secure with a cocktail stick. Place on the griddle and cook for 8 minutes, turning the scallops to give the bacon an even colour.

2 Shell the eggs carefully. Toss the mixed leaf salad in a large serving dish with the olive oil, lemon juice and seasoning, to taste.

3 When the scallops are cooked, arrange them on top of the salad. Finally, break the soft-boiled eggs in half, add to the salad and serve quickly before all the yolk runs out. Garnish with lemon rind and snipped chives.

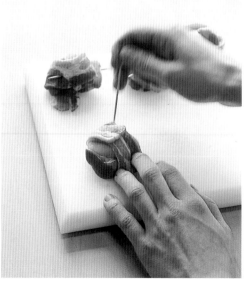

FOOD FACT • Scallops are sold fresh in the shell or ready-shelled. If you are buying the latter, choose ones that are creamy ivory in colour as opposed to very white and that have a bright orange coral. If you buy scallops in the shell you will need to prepare them before cooking. Lever the shells apart using a strong knife, sliding the knife underneath the tough muscle holding the scallop to the flat half of the shell. Carefully rinse the scallop still in the rounded half of the shell under cold running water, removing the membrane around it. Slit open the coral with a sharp pointed knife and remove the dark vein and the attached black intestinal bag. Ease the scallop free from the shell. The white flesh, and the orange coral attached to it, are now ready to cook.

Swordfish with Shellfish

Griddling is such a pure way to cook these ingredients as all the flavours are kept very simple.

Serves: **4**

Preparation time: 10 minutes

Cooking time: 20–25 minutes

4 x 150 g/5 oz swordfish steaks or fillets
100 g/3½ oz mussels, scrubbed and debearded
100 g/3½ oz raw green prawns, peeled and
   deveined
100 g/3½ oz clams, scrubbed and debearded
8 tablespoons lemon juice
1 bunch of flat leaf parsley, chopped, plus extra
   to garnish
2 garlic cloves, crushed
100 ml/3½ fl oz white wine
sea salt and pepper
grated lemon rind, to garnish

1 Heat the griddle pan. Place the swordfish pieces on to cook for 5 minutes on each side. When cooked, place the swordfish in a low oven to keep warm.

2 Add the mussels (discarding any that are open), green prawns and clams to the griddle pan and cook for 10 minutes, moving them around. All the mussels and clams should open up during cooking. Discard any shells that do not.

3 Add the lemon juice, chopped parsley, garlic and white wine to the shellfish in the griddle pan and simmer for 2 minutes. Arrange the griddled swordfish pieces on individual plates and spoon the shellfish over the top. Season with salt and pepper, garnish with lemon rind and chopped parsley and serve at once.

King Prawns with Pineapple

The pineapple needs to be cut lengthways into strips for these deliciously fruity kebab-style prawns, which make impressive nibbling food or a special starter.

Serves: **4**

Preparation time: 15 minutes

Cooking time: 10 minutes

12 tarragon sprigs
12 raw king prawns, heads removed
  and deveined, tails left intact
12 long thin slices of pineapple

1 Heat the griddle pan. Place a sprig of tarragon on top of each prawn and wrap with a thin ribbon of pineapple; secure with a cocktail stick.

2 Place on the griddle and cook the wrapped prawns for 5 minutes on each side. Serve the prawns hot or cold.

FOOD FACT • Tarragon is a strong-flavoured aromatic herb, of which there are two varieties. French tarragon, which tastes of vanilla and aniseed, is superior to the Russian variety, which has a duller flavour and a coarser, narrower leaf. Tarragon is most often used with egg dishes, chicken and fish.

Griddled Scallops in Their Shells

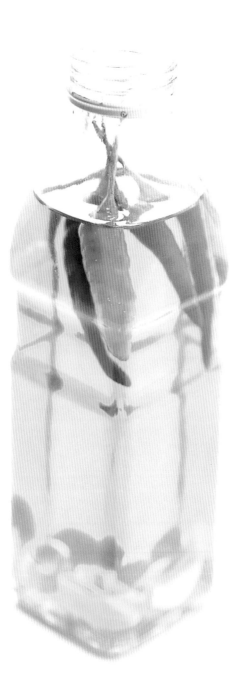

Serve these attractive shellfish as an appetizer to go with drinks. Cook them to order for your friends and don't be shy – let them watch you make these simple delicacies!

Serves: **4**

Preparation time: 5 minutes

Cooking time: 2–4 minutes

12 large scallops (see page 112)
4 tablespoons lime juice
olive oil infused with chilli and garlic, for drizzling
sea salt and black pepper
TO GARNISH
lime rind strips
finely sliced chillies (optional)

1 Heat the griddle pan. Pat the scallops dry with kitchen paper. Griddle the scallops for 1–2 minutes on each side then remove from the pan. Do not overcook them or they will become tough.

2 Divide the scallops between 4 cleaned scallop shells or small serving plates. Drizzle with the lime juice and a little chilli and garlic olive oil, and season with salt and pepper. Garnish with strips of lime rind and sliced chillies, if using.

FOOD FACT • Olive oil infused with flavourings such as chilli, garlic, sun-dried tomatoes, peppercorns, lemons and herbs is now widely available. However, it is very easy to make your own. Simply drop your chosen flavouring into a bottle of good-quality olive oil and leave to infuse for a couple of weeks before using, to allow the flavour to permeate the oil. Such flavoured oils are best used in salad dressings and other cold preparations since heating can greatly reduce their flavour and aroma.

Oriental Griddled Prawn Salad

This salad is really tasty and fresh as all the vegetables are raw. Add more of your favourites to make your own personally tailored salad.

Serves: **4**

Preparation time: 10 minutes

Cooking time: 4–6 minutes

16 raw king or tiger prawns, peeled and
    deveined
100 g/3½ oz bean sprouts
1 bunch of chives
1 shallot, finely chopped
1 red chilli, finely chopped
4 cm/1½ inch piece of fresh root ginger, peeled
    and finely chopped
2.5 cm/1 inch piece of galangal, peeled and
    finely chopped
2 garlic cloves, finely chopped
2–4 tablespoons sweet chilli sauce
4 tablespoons lime juice
50 g/2 oz peanuts, chopped
lime rind, to garnish

1 Heat the griddle pan. Cut the prawns in half lengthways and place on the griddle; cook for 2–3 minutes on each side.

2 Place the bean sprouts in a serving bowl. Cut the chives into long lengths and add to the bowl with the finely chopped shallot. Add the chopped chilli, ginger, galangal and garlic to the bowl, together with the sweet chilli sauce, adjusting the quantity to taste, and lime juice. Mix well to blend all the flavours.

3 Arrange the salad on individual plates. Place the griddled prawns on top, sprinkle over the chopped peanuts and serve with a lime rind spiral, to garnish.

FOOD FACT • Galangal is a root similar in appearance to ginger but lighter in colour and tinged with pink. It has a wonderful aroma and flavour – combining ginger, pine and citrus – and is an important ingredient in Thai and Malaysian cooking. Like ginger, it is used thinly sliced or chopped or in powder form and is available from oriental stores.

Crayfish with Spicy Butter

Crayfish are a real treat and this recipe is ideal for a splendid special occasion meal for two.

Serves: **2**

Preparation time: 10 minutes

Cooking time: 30–45 minutes

1 kg/2 lb crayfish
SPICY BUTTER
100 g/3½ oz butter, at room temperature
½ tablespoon paprika
1 red chilli, deseeded and finely chopped
1 green chilli, deseeded and finely chopped
1 garlic clove, finely chopped
grated rind of ½ lemon
TO GARNISH
grated lemon rind
chopped parsley

1 Remove the heads from the crayfish and cut them in half lengthways, shell and all, using a sharp knife – a good fishmonger will do this for you.

2 Heat the griddle and place a batch of crayfish on to cook for 10–15 minutes in total, depending on their size. The shells will turn pink and the flesh becomes firm and white. Remove the crayfish from the griddle when cooked and keep warm while you cook the remaining crayfish in the same way.

3 Meanwhile, cut the butter into small pieces and place in a bowl. Add the paprika, chilli, garlic and lemon rind and mix well.

4 When all the crayfish have been cooked arrange the pieces on 2 serving bowls or plates. Divide the butter mixture in half and spoon on top of the hot crayfish. Serve immediately, garnished with lemon rind and chopped parsley.

FOOD FACT • Crayfish are freshwater crustacea, which look like small lobsters and vary in colour from dark purple to black. They are sold both live and ready-cooked. Most of the flesh of a crayfish is in the tail.
The bitter-tasting intestinal tube under the tail needs removing. This can be done before or after cooking, using a sharp knife, or by twisting off the middle tail fin, which will bring the intestine with it.

Chicken

Chicken Strips with Prosciutto and Rosemary

This chicken wrapped in prosciutto can be served hot or cold. It is a particularly good recipe for serving in the summer and for producing on picnics. Roasted vine tomatoes and a mixed salad dressed with balsamic vinegar and olive oil make perfect accompaniments.

Serves: **4**

Preparation time: 10 minutes

Cooking time: 20 minutes

4 x 100 g/3½ oz skinless chicken breasts
8 large slices of prosciutto
rosemary sprigs
sea salt and pepper

1 Heat the griddle pan. Cut the chicken breasts in half lengthways.

2 Lay out the prosciutto on a board. Place a piece of chicken on top of each piece of prosciutto, add a few sprigs of rosemary and season. Wrap the prosciutto around the chicken to enclose it fully.

3 Place the wrapped chicken on the griddle and cook for 20 minutes in total, turning so that the prosciutto does not burn. Reduce the heat if it is too fierce. Serve hot or cold.

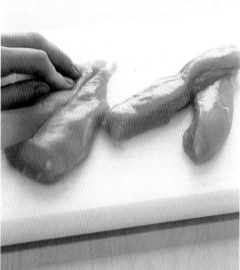
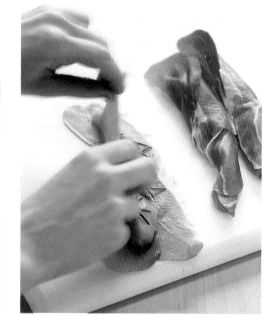

FOOD FACT • 'Prosciutto' simply means ham in Italy. Outside Italy, however, it means raw ham, the best of which comes from Parma. Parma ham is lightly salted and best recognized as the transparently thin slices served with fresh melon or figs as a starter.

Chicken Stacks

This simple yet impressive recipe combines griddled chicken with Parma ham and melting fontina cheese for a scrumptious medley of flavours and textures. Serve with freshly cooked pasta, tossed with butter and black pepper.

Serves: **4**

Preparation time: 10 minutes

Cooking time: 50–55 minutes

Oven temperature: 180°C/350°F/Gas Mark 4

4 x 125 g/4 oz skinless chicken fillets
1 small bunch of sage
4 slices of prosciutto
4 slices of fontina cheese, rind removed
olive oil, for drizzling
sea salt and pepper

1 Heat the griddle pan. Lay the chicken fillets flat on a board and, using a sharp knife, slice each one horizontally to give 3 flat pieces.

2 Griddle 4 pieces of chicken for 5 minutes on each side. When cooked, arrange these on an oiled baking sheet – these will form the base of the stacks. Put a few sage leaves on top of each one and season.

3 Cut each length of prosciutto in half and griddle 4 pieces for 4 minutes on each side. Place these on top of the griddled chicken. Cut each slice of fontina in half. Top each chicken and prosciutto stack with a piece of cheese.

4 Griddle the remaining chicken and prosciutto and stack up as before with the cheese and sage, completing each stack with a final layer of chicken. Place the baking sheet in a preheated oven, 180°C/350°F/Gas Mark 4, and cook until the cheese is soft, about 5–8 minutes. Drizzle with a little olive oil, sprinkle with salt and pepper and garnish with a few sage leaves. Serve with freshly cooked pasta tossed in butter and black pepper.

FOOD FACT • Fontina is a fat, rich, semi-soft, smooth cheese, which is made from cows' milk and is slightly elastic. It melts beautifully, has a nutty flavour similar to Gruyère and is dotted with small holes. The cheese is made in flat wheel shapes and has a natural rind.

Cypriot Chicken and Haloumi Salad

Haloumi is a wonderful cheese for griddling, grilling or frying. Here it provides a lovely contrast of texture for the chunky Mediterranean salad and oregano-marinated chicken.

Serves: **4**

Preparation time: 20 minutes, plus marinating

Cooking time: 23–28 minutes

3 x 125 g/4 oz skinless chicken fillets,
  cut into chunks
1 bunch of oregano, chopped
1 tablespoon olive oil
250 g/8 oz haloumi cheese
sea salt and pepper

CYPRIOT SALAD

1 cucumber, skinned and deseeded
4 beefsteak tomatoes, skinned, deseeded
  and cut into wedges
1 red onion, finely chopped
1 bunch of flat-leaf parsley, roughly chopped
3 tablespoons olive oil
1 tablespoon wine vinegar
sea salt and pepper

1 Place the chunks of chicken in a bowl. Add the chopped oregano, olive oil and seasoning. Allow to marinate at room temperature for 2 hours.

2 Heat the griddle pan. Add the marinated chicken and cook for 15–20 minutes, turning to achieve a good colour all over. When cooked, remove from the griddle and keep warm.

3 While the chicken is cooking, make the salad. Cut the cucumber lengthways into short battens. Place in a bowl and add the tomato wedges, chopped red onion and parsley. Add the olive oil and wine vinegar. Toss well and season to taste.

4 Slice the haloumi into 8 and griddle the slices for 4 minutes on each side then serve with the chicken and salad.

Moroccan Chicken

In typical Moroccan fashion, this recipe involves rubbing the chicken with pungent spices and herbs before cooking so that it is well flavoured. Paprika, cumin seeds and fresh coriander are all typical Moroccan ingredients.

Serves: **4**

Preparation time: 10 minutes

Cooking time: 20 minutes

1 onion, very finely chopped
2 teaspoons paprika
1 teaspoon cumin seeds
4 x 125 g/4 oz skinless chicken fillets
1 bunch of coriander, finely chopped
4 tablespoons lemon juice
3 tablespoons olive oil
sea salt and pepper
TO SERVE
Harissa (see page 226)
freshly boiled rice

1 Heat the griddle pan. Place the onion in a bowl. Add the paprika and cumin seeds and mix together. Rub the onion and spice mixture into the chicken fillets.

2 Cook the chicken on the griddle for 10 minutes on each side, turning once. When cooked, remove from the pan.

3 Place the finely chopped coriander in a bowl and add the lemon juice, olive oil and a little seasoning. Add the chicken to the bowl and toss well. Serve accompanied by a bowl of harissa and boiled rice.

Griddled Chicken Fajitas

Serve these fajitas ready assembled or, alternatively, serve all the different ingredients separately in bowls at the table and allow everyone to assemble their own fajita. Supply chilled bottles of Mexican beer to drink and tortilla chips to go with the meal.

Serves: **4**

Preparation time: 20 minutes, plus marinating

Cooking time: 15–20 minutes

4 x 125 g/4 oz skinless chicken fillets
4 large soft tortillas
150 ml/¼ pint soured cream
4 tomatoes, skinned and sliced
1 avocado, sliced
4 spring onions, sliced
½ red onion, sliced
sea salt and pepper
tortilla chips, to serve (optional)
MARINADE
2 tablespoons soy sauce
3 cm/1¼ inch piece of fresh root ginger, finely chopped
2 garlic cloves, finely chopped
2 tablespoons olive oil
1 bunch of coriander, chopped
1 chilli, chopped
2 tablespoons lime juice

1 Combine all the ingredients for the marinade – the soy sauce, ginger, garlic, olive oil, coriander, chilli and lime juice – in a shallow dish. Add the chicken fillets and leave to marinate at room temperature for 2 hours, or in the fridge for 24 hours.

2 Heat the griddle pan. Place the marinated chicken fillets on to cook for 7–10 minutes on each side. When cooked, remove the chicken from the pan and slice it into long strips.

3 Place the tortillas under a preheated grill and cook for 30 seconds on each side. Spread over one side of each, a spoonful of soured cream, a little sliced tomato, sliced avocado and a sprinkling of sliced spring onions and red onion.

4 Finally, add the pieces of griddled chicken and season. Roll up each tortilla tightly and cut in half across each one. Serve with tortilla chips, if liked.

FOOD FACT • A tortilla is a traditional, circular, flat unleavened Mexican bread, made from corn or wheat flour. Tortillas can be served in a variety of ways – plain or buttered, filled and rolled – as here – or folded and fried. Popular accompaniments for fajitas include extra soured cream and guacamole – a dish of seasoned mashed avocado.

Chicken Satay Sticks

Soak the wooden skewers in water for 30 minutes before use to prevent them burning during cooking.

Serves: **4**

Preparation time: 10 minutes, plus marinating

Cooking time: 20 minutes

4 x 125 g/4 oz skinless chicken fillets
chopped coriander, to garnish
MARINADE
4 tablespoons soy sauce
4 tablespoons lime juice
1 garlic clove, crushed
1 teaspoon curry powder
1 teaspoon peanut butter
pinch of dried chilli flakes
SATAY SAUCE
1 tablespoon peanut butter
2 tablespoons lime juice
1 teaspoon curry powder
1 garlic clove, crushed
4 tablespoons water

1 Combine all the marinade ingredients in a shallow dish. Mix until smooth.

2 Cut each skinless chicken fillet lengthways into 3 strips. Thread the pieces of chicken on to 12 presoaked wooden skewers. Place in the dish of marinade, coat well and leave to marinate at room temperature for up to 2 hours.

3 To make the sauce, combine the peanut butter, lime juice, curry powder, garlic and water in a small bowl. Blend until smooth.

4 Heat the griddle pan. Cook the chicken sticks in batches for 5 minutes on each side. Keep them warm while you cook the remainder. Serve garnished with chopped coriander and with plenty of the satay sauce for dipping.

Indonesian Chicken with Grilled Bananas

This may sound an unusual combination but in Indonesia bananas are frequently served as part of a savoury meal. This dish goes very well with a stir-fry of vegetables and sesame seeds.

Serves: **4**

Preparation time: 10 minutes, plus marinating

Cooking time: 20 minutes

1 Mix together all the spices and the salt in a shallow dish. Add the chicken fillets, rub the mixture in well and cover and leave to marinate at room temperature for 2 hours.

2 Heat the griddle pan. Meanwhile, cut the bananas in half lengthways, leaving the skin on. Sprinkle the banana flesh with the brown sugar, place under a preheated grill and cook for 3–4 minutes. Turn the grill off but leave the bananas in the decreasing warmth.

3 Place the chicken fillets on the griddle pan and cook for 7 minutes on each side. Remove and serve immediately with the grilled bananas and a vegetable stir-fry, if liked.

½ teaspoon ground ginger
1 teaspoon cayenne pepper
½ teaspoon allspice
½ teaspoon cinnamon
1 teaspoon curry powder
1 teaspoon paprika
½ teaspoon turmeric
½ teaspoon sea salt
4 x 125 g/4 oz skinless chicken fillets
2 bananas
1 tablespoon light brown sugar
vegetable stir-fry, to serve (optional)

Lemon-infused Chicken and Spaghetti

Serves: **4**

Preparation time: 15 minutes

Cooking time: 16 minutes

4 lemons
4 x 125 g/4 oz skinless chicken fillets
1 bunch of oregano, chopped
300 g/10 oz spaghetti
1 bunch of parsley, chopped
2 tablespoons olive oil
sea salt and pepper

1 Thinly slice 3 of the lemons, setting aside 8 large slices. Grate the rind and squeeze the juice from the fourth lemon, and set aside.

2 Using a sharp knife, make a pouch in the middle of each chicken fillet. Fill each chicken pocket with the smaller slices of lemon, some chopped oregano leaves and salt and pepper.

3 Heat the griddle pan. Sandwich each chicken fillet between 2 of the reserved large lemon slices and a sprig of oregano. Place the chicken on the griddle and cook for 8 minutes on each side – try to keep the lemon intact with the chicken so that all the citrus flavour infuses into the chicken.

4 Meanwhile, bring a large saucepan of lightly salted water to the boil. When boiling, plunge the spaghetti into the water and cook for 12 minutes, or according to packet instructions. Drain well, then toss with the grated rind and lemon juice, the chopped parsley, olive oil and seasoning. Serve with the lemon chicken.

Szechuan Chicken

Serves: **4**

Preparation time: 5 minutes, plus marinating

Cooking time: 14–20 minutes

3 tablespoons soy sauce
2 tablespoons dry sherry
1 teaspoon rice vinegar
3 cm/1¼ inch piece of fresh root ginger,
  finely chopped
1 garlic clove, crushed
1 tablespoon Chinese chilli paste
½ teaspoon Szechuan peppercorns, ground
1 tablespoon dark sesame oil
4 x 125 g/4 oz skinless chicken fillets
coriander, to garnish
TO SERVE
soba noodles
stir-fried oyster mushrooms

1 Mix together all the ingredients, except the chicken, in a shallow dish to make the marinade. Add the chicken fillets, coat well with the marinade and allow to marinate at room temperature for 2 hours.

2 Heat the griddle pan. Cook the chicken on the griddle for 7–10 minutes on each side and garnish with chopped coriander. Serve with soba noodles and stir-fried oyster mushrooms.

FOOD FACT • Szechuan, or anise, peppercorns are the dried red berries of a small Chinese shrub. The spice has a hot, aromatic flavour and is an ingredient in Chinese five-spice powder. Nothing happens when you first bite it, then the spice floods your mouth with a strong, hot, almost numbing effect.

Griddled Tandoori Chicken

Traditionally, tandoori is an Indian style of cooking, based on a charcoal-heated clay oven, a tandoor, *where the intense heat cooks food quickly, lightly charring its surface while keeping it tender and moist within. Here, the same effect is reproduced on a griddle.*

4 x 125 g/4 oz skinless chicken fillets
4 tablespoons tandoori paste or powder
2 red onions, finely sliced
4 tomatoes, finely sliced
1 bunch of coriander, roughly chopped
4 tablespoons lemon juice
4 tablespoons olive oil
sea salt and pepper
griddled lemon wedges, to serve

Serves: **4**

Preparation time: 10 minutes, plus marinating

Cooking time: 16–20 minutes

1 Using a sharp knife, make a series of small slashes in the flesh of the chicken fillets and rub in the tandoori paste or powder. Leave to marinate in the refrigerator overnight.

2 Heat the griddle pan. Place the marinated chicken fillets on to cook for 8–10 minutes on each side, allowing the authentic tandoori charred colour to appear.

3 Mix the red onions, tomatoes and coriander together with the lemon juice, olive oil and seasoning in a small bowl. Serve the salad with the tandoori chicken, accompanied by griddled lemon wedges.

Chicken with Chilli Jam

Don't forget to wash your hands thoroughly after chopping the chillies as they will burn or, better still, wear rubber gloves.

Serves: **4**

Preparation time: 5 minutes

Cooking time: 25 minutes

4 x 125 g/4 oz boneless chicken breasts
rice noodles, to serve
coriander leaves, to garnish
CHILLI JAM
125 g/4 oz fresh chillies, cored, deseeded
    and chopped
1 garlic clove, crushed
1 onion, chopped
5 cm/2 inch piece of fresh root ginger,
    peeled and chopped
125 ml/4 fl oz white vinegar
500 g/1 lb sugar

1 First make the chilli jam. Place the chopped chillies, the garlic, chopped onion and ginger in a small saucepan. Add the white vinegar and sugar. Bring to the boil, then reduce the heat and allow to simmer for 15 minutes. The mixture should be thick, sticky and jam-like, and will become more so as it cools.

2 Meanwhile, heat the griddle pan. Place the chicken breasts on the griddle, skin side down, and cook for 10 minutes. Turn the chicken over and cook for a further 10 minutes.

3 Serve the chicken on a bed of noodles, with the chilli jam poured over the top, and garnish with coriander. Store any remaining chilli jam in the refrigerator, covered, for up to 1 week, and use it as an accompaniment to spice up other griddled meats.

Devilled Chicken

Serves: **4**

Preparation time: 10 minutes

Cooking time: 35–40 minutes

8 boneless chicken thighs
dressed salad leaves, to serve
DEVIL SAUCE
2 tablespoons Dijon mustard
6 drops of Tabasco sauce
2 garlic cloves, crushed
1 tablespoon soy sauce

1 Heat the griddle pan. Open out the chicken thighs, trim away any fat and remove the skin.

2 To make the devil sauce, mix together the Dijon mustard, Tabasco sauce, garlic and soy sauce in a shallow dish. Dip the trimmed chicken thighs in the devil sauce and coat each piece well all over.

3 Place the chicken pieces flat on the griddle and cook for 8–10 minutes on each side. Serve hot or cold with dressed salad leaves.

FOOD FACT • The main ingredient in Devil sauce, Dijon mustard is a famous French mustard from Dijon, which is considered the 'capital' of mustard production. It is made from brown mustard seeds blended with salt, spices and white wine or wine vinegar. It is pale in colour, either smooth or coarse-grained, and fairly hot and sharp-tasting.

Griddled Summer Chicken Salad

Serve this hearty salad with warm crusty bread. You will find the chunks of chicken combined with griddled seasonal asparagus never fails to satisfy.

Serves: **4**

Preparation time: 15 minutes

Cooking time: 45 minutes

4 x 125 g/4 oz skinless chicken fillets
2 small red onions
2 red peppers, cored, deseeded and cut
   into flat pieces
1 bunch of asparagus, trimmed
200 g/7 oz boiled new potatoes, cut in half
1 bunch of basil
5 tablespoons olive oil
2 tablespoons balsamic vinegar
sea salt and pepper

1 Heat the griddle pan. Place the chicken fillets on the griddle and cook for 10 minutes on each side. When cooked, remove from the griddle and cut roughly into chunks.

2 Cut the red onions into wedges, keeping the root ends intact to hold the wedges together. Place on the griddle and cook for 5 minutes on each side. Remove from the pan and set aside.

3 Place the flat pieces of red pepper on the griddle and cook for 8 minutes on the skin side only, so that the skins are charred and blistered. Remove and set aside, then cook the asparagus on the griddle for 6 minutes, turning frequently.

4 Place the potatoes in a large bowl. Tear the basil, reserving a few leaves intact to garnish, and add to the bowl, together with the griddled chicken and all the vegetables. Add the olive oil, balsamic vinegar and seasoning. Toss the salad and serve garnished with the reserved basil leaves.

Oriental Chicken Cakes

Serves: **4**

Preparation time: 15 minutes

Cooking time: 16 minutes

575 g/1 lb 3 oz minced chicken or turkey
1 lemon grass stalk, very finely chopped
2 kaffir lime leaves, very finely chopped
5 cm/2 inch piece of fresh root ginger,
  very finely chopped
2 green chillies, very finely chopped
2 garlic cloves, very finely chopped
1 egg, beaten
1 tablespoon sesame seeds, toasted
  (see page 86)
TO SERVE
rice noodles
chopped peanuts
sliced onion
bean sprouts
chopped coriander
Chilli Jam (see page 146)

1 Place the minced chicken or turkey in a large bowl. Add the finely chopped lemon grass, kaffir lime leaves, ginger, chilli and garlic, which need to be so finely chopped as to almost make a paste. Add the beaten egg and sesame seeds. Mix well, using your hands.

2 Heat the griddle pan. Divide the mixture into 8 and shape into small patties. Place on the griddle and cook for 8 minutes on each side.

3 Serve the chicken cakes with a salad of rice noodles, chopped peanuts, sliced onion, bean sprouts and lots of chopped coriander, accompanied by chilli jam.

FOOD FACT • Kaffir lime leaves are glossy and dark green with a strong lemon–lime flavour and scent. The leaves grow in pairs and their full citrus flavour is imparted when they are torn or shredded. They are common ingredients in Thai, Malaysian and Indonesian cooking. They are available fresh or dried; fresh kaffir lime leaves may be frozen for later use.

Chicken with Peanut Sauce

Serve this simple but delicious dish with a noodle and vegetable stir-fry tossed in sesame oil.

Serves: **4**

Preparation time: 5 minutes

Cooking time: 16 minutes

4 x 125 g/4 oz boneless chicken breasts
1 tablespoon soy sauce
2 tablespoons crunchy or smooth
  peanut butter
4 tablespoons lemon juice
4 tablespoons water
pepper
TO GARNISH
coriander leaves
chopped fried peanuts (optional)

1 Heat the griddle pan. Place the chicken breasts on the griddle and cook for 8 minutes on each side.

2 Meanwhile, place the soy sauce, peanut butter, lemon juice, water and a little pepper in a small saucepan. Mix well and heat gently, adjusting the consistency of the sauce with a little more water if necessary, so that is slightly runny but coats the back of a spoon.

3 When the chicken is cooked, serve with the peanut sauce drizzled over the top, garnished with coriander and chopped fried peanuts, if liked.

Duck &
Other
Poultry

Griddled Turkey Burgers

These burgers are ideal for people concerned with a healthy diet since turkey is so low in saturated fat.

Serves: **4**

Preparation time: 20 minutes

Cooking time: 12–20 minutes

700 g/1 lb 7 oz minced turkey
1 shallot, finely chopped, plus extra to garnish
1 bunch of thyme, chopped
½ teaspoon Worcestershire sauce
3 drops of Tabasco sauce
2 egg yolks
1 ciabatta loaf
Dijon mustard, for spreading
mayonnaise, for spreading
2 tomatoes, sliced
1 bag of herb salad leaves
sea salt and pepper

1 Place the minced turkey in a large bowl. Add the chopped shallot, thyme, Worcestershire and Tabasco sauces and egg yolks. Season to taste and mix well.

2 Heat the griddle pan. Using your hands, divide the turkey mixture into 4. Shape into patties and place them on the griddle to cook for 6–10 minutes on each side, depending on the thickness of the patties.

3 Cut the ciabatta in half horizontally and toast the 2 lengths under a preheated grill. Cut each piece in half. Spread the ciabatta with mustard and mayonnaise. Top with tomato slices and herb salad leaves, finally adding the griddled turkey burgers on top. Garnish with a little chopped thyme, if liked.

Griddled Duck with Green Mango Salad

Here, the richness of the duck is beautifully balanced by the refreshing taste of the mango salad – always a success.

Serves: **4**

Preparation time: 10 minutes

Cooking time: 20 minutes

4 x 200 g/7 oz duck breasts
2 green mangoes (see page 240)
1 garlic clove, very finely chopped
3 cm/1¼ inch piece of fresh root ginger, very finely chopped
1 green chilli, very finely chopped
50 g/2 oz bean sprouts
2 heads of pak choi, sliced (see page 94)
1 bunch of spring onions, diagonally sliced
4 tablespoons lime juice
1 tablespoon rice vinegar
2 tablespoons vegetable oil

1 Heat the griddle pan. Using a fork, pierce the skin of the duck breasts – the more times you do it, the better the breast will be as it allows the fat to run out and makes the duck skin crispy.

2 Place the duck breasts on the griddle, skin side down, and cook for 10 minutes. If necessary, drain off some of the cooking fat and then turn the duck over and cook for 5 minutes on the other side. Finally, turn the duck back to the skin side for the final crisping. Allow to cool slightly, then carve into thin slices.

3 Peel the green mangoes and grate or slice into a bowl. Add the very finely chopped garlic, ginger and chilli, followed by the bean sprouts. Add the sliced pak choi to the mango salad with the spring onions. Mix well. Finally, add the lime juice, rice vinegar and vegetable oil and mix again.

4 Arrange the mango salad on individual plates and top with the sliced, griddled duck to serve.

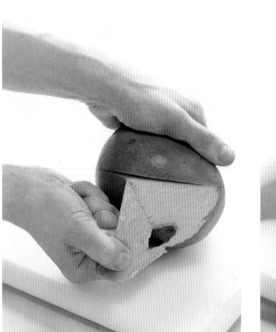

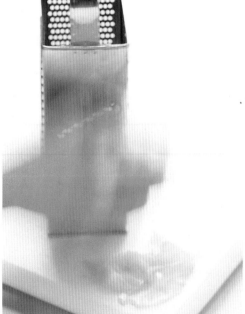

Ostrich with Mushrooms and Spiced Butter

Serves: **4**

Preparation time: 10 minutes

Cooking time: 15–25 minutes

4 large open cap mushrooms, stalks removed
4 x 175 g/6 oz ostrich steaks or fillets
parsley, to garnish
roasted vine tomatoes (see page 220), to serve
SPICED BUTTER
2 shallots, very finely chopped
2 garlic cloves, crushed and finely chopped
1 bunch of parsley, chopped
75 g/3 oz butter, softened
1 teaspoon Worcestershire sauce

1 Heat the griddle pan. Add the mushrooms, gills facing down, and cook for 5 minutes. Turn the mushrooms over and cook for another 5 minutes. Place the mushrooms in a low oven to keep warm.

2 To make the spiced butter, mix the shallots in a small bowl with the garlic, parsley, butter, Worcestershire sauce and seasoning.

3 Place the ostrich steaks on the griddle and cook for 3–4 minutes on each side for rare, 5 minutes for medium or 7 minutes for well done. To serve, arrange the mushrooms on individual plates, add the griddled ostrich steaks and finally the spiced butter, divided between the 4 servings. Garnish with parsley and serve with roasted tomatoes.

FOOD FACT • Ostrich meat is becoming increasingly widely available. It tastes like slightly sweet beef and, because it is a very lean meat, is best served with a sauce, as here, to add a little moisture.

Duck with Spiced Fruits

Serves: **4**

Preparation time: 15 minutes

Cooking time: 25 minutes

1 cooking apple, peeled, cored and chopped
100 ml/3½ fl oz orange juice
2 star anise
1 dessert apple, cored and cut into wedges
1 pear, cored and cut into wedges
25 g/1 oz butter
4 x 200 g/7 oz duck breasts
4 tablespoons balsamic vinegar

1 Place the chopped cooking apple in a small saucepan with the orange juice and star anise and cook over a gentle heat until the apple is soft – about 4 minutes.

2 Add the dessert apple and pear wedges to the soft cooked apple with the butter. Mix well, cover the pan and leave on a gentle heat for 2 minutes, then turn off the heat and leave the pan covered.

3 Heat the griddle pan. Using a fork, pierce the skin of the duck breasts – the more times you do it, the better the breast will be as this allows the fat to run out and make the duck skin crispy.

4 Place the duck breasts on the griddle, skin side down, and cook for 12 minutes. If necessary, drain off some of the cooking fat, and then turn the duck over and cook for 5 minutes on the other side, pouring the balsamic vinegar over the duck for the final 20 seconds of cooking.

5 Heat the spiced fruit sauce and serve with the griddled duck breast.

FOOD FACT • Star anise is the attractive dried, star-shaped fruit of a small evergreen tree native to China. It is red-brown in colour with a pungent aniseed flavour and is an ingredient in Chinese five-spice powder. It is widely used in Chinese cooking, particularly with pork and duck.

Turkey Tacos with Hot Green Salsa

This dish is very versatile as it can be served hot or cold. If you prefer, chop the turkey finely, mix it with the salsa and use as a tasty sandwich filling. The salsa ingredients can all be chopped by hand or they can be processed in a blender for a smoother texture. Sometimes time is a big factor in this but the hand-chopped version is probably preferable and certainly more authentic.

Serves: **4**

Preparation time: 10 minutes

Cooking time: 16 minutes

4 x 175 g/6 oz turkey fillets
HOT GREEN SALSA
1 avocado, chopped
1 red onion, finely chopped
1–2 hot green or red chillies, very finely chopped
1 garlic clove, very finely chopped
1 bunch of coriander, roughly chopped
4 tablespoons lime juice
4 tablespoons olive oil
sea salt and pepper
TO SERVE
16 taco shells
150 ml/¼ pint soured cream

1 Heat the griddle pan. Place the turkey fillets on the griddle and cook for 8 minutes on each side. Remove from the pan and slice into strips.

2 To make the salsa, place the chopped avocado in a bowl and add the red onion, chilli, garlic and coriander. Mix together, adding the lime juice, olive oil and seasoning.

3 To assemble the dish, pile some of the salsa in each of the taco shells and top with a few strips of turkey. Serve the remaining salsa separately, with a bowl of soured cream to spoon on top of the tacos just before eating.

FOOD FACT • The avocado is a tropical fruit-vegetable, of which there are two main varieties. One has a warty purple-black skin when ripe; the other is more pear shaped and is smooth and dark green in colour. To determine whether the latter is ripe, cup it lightly in one hand and squeeze very gently. If it gives slightly under pressure, the avocado is ready to eat.

Red & White Meat

Griddled poultry or meat is an obvious choice for a simple, tasty main course. For the most attractive effect, slap it on the preheated griddle at an angle so that the char lines run diagonally across the meat. For a criss-cross effect, rotate the piece through an angle of 45° or 90° halfway through cooking each side.

Poultry

Poultry is one of the most versatile foods for griddling, accepting almost any marinade or sauce with beautiful results. Chicken and turkey fillets are particularly ideal.

Chicken and duck
Chicken breasts have become the food for modern living – quick and easy to prepare, and enjoyed by most people, and yet, chicken is all too often bland. Choose organic, corn-fed or free-range fresh chicken for the best flavour. Frozen chicken can be characterless and needs more attention in the way of flavouring. Frozen duck is not so bad since its greater fat content compared with that of chicken assures that, when defrosted, duck retains its succulence and the stronger flavour is not so easily frozen out.

Turkey
Turkey is so lean that it can easily dry out when griddled. If you cook it straight from the refrigerator, rather than letting it come to room temperature, it will be less likely to overcook.

Meat on the griddle

When griddling meat, take care when you season it. Salt should only be added towards the end of the cooking time as it draws moisture to the outside of the meat, inhibiting searing and browning.

The thicker the cut of meat, the more gently it should be cooked after the initial searing. The ideal thickness for steaks or lean slices of meat is 1–1.5 cm/ ½–¾ inch thick. Very thin slices of meat should be cooked over a high heat and will take only about 1 minute each side. Thick slices of meat, more than 1 cm/½ inch thick, should be sealed over a high heat, then cooked over a low heat. Cooking times are around the same as for pan-frying or barbecuing. Always allow griddled meat to rest for a few minutes after cooking so that the juices will be evenly distributed throughout the flesh.

Beef
The tenderness of a cut of beef determines whether it can be griddled or not. The internal fat which marbles the meat keeps the flesh moist as the outside chars to a crisp, succulent crust. Tender cuts of beef – primarily from the loin, such as fillet and sirloin – are all ideal for griddling. These are tender enough to be cooked without a marinade although a marinade does give extra flavour. Other cuts of beef will need a tenderizing marinade first if they are to be griddled, although there are differing opinions on the importance of this (see page 8).

Pork

Pork accepts marinades beautifully and tends to stay moist during cooking because of its high internal fat content. Fresh rather than frozen pork is best for griddling. The cell walls in meat break down during freezing causing significant water loss and dryer tasteless meat when cooked. Pork should be cooked until well done, but not dried out since it can be ruined by overcooking.

Lamb

Lamb is a natural for griddling because the excess fat drips off during cooking and can be tipped away. Lamb fillet, rib and loin chops are the most popular cuts for griddling. The chops are tender and require no marinade. For tasty kebabs, use chunks from the shoulder or leg and marinate them.

Veal

Veal contains no internal marbling and very little external fat. It can, therefore, be dry and has very little natural flavour, but accepts the flavour of marinades well. It is most often served with a rich sauce. The best escalopes are those cut from the fillet end of the leg. You can pound the escalopes yourself for extra tenderness, by carefully using a rolling pin.

Griddled Turkey and Mango

This is a great dish for a summer garden party. Instead of stacking the griddled turkey and mango slices as here, simply chop them into chunks once cooked, toss in a large bowl with the passion fruit dressing and serve.

Serves: **4**

Preparation time: 15 minutes

Cooking time: 40 minutes

4 x 175 g/6 oz turkey escalopes
2 mangoes (see page 240)
3 passion fruits
3 tablespoons olive oil
1 tablespoon white wine vinegar
sea salt and pepper
wild and long grain rice, tossed with
  herbs, to serve

1 Lay each turkey escalope between 2 pieces of clingfilm and flatten with a wooden mallet or a rolling pin. Try and get the escalopes as thin as possible – about 5 mm/¼ inch. Cut each fillet into 3 even-sized pieces.

2 Heat the griddle pan. Peel the skin from each mango and cut 3 slices from either side of the stone. Place the mango slices on the griddle and cook for 4 minutes on each side, or until the mango has griddle marks. Remove and keep warm in a low oven.

3 Place the flattened turkey pieces on the griddle and cook in batches for 5 minutes on each side. Keep the griddled pieces warm while you cook the remainder.

4 Cut the passion fruit in half, scoop out the seeds and place in a bowl. Add the olive oil, vinegar and seasoning and mix well.

5 To serve, stack the slices of turkey and mango in alternate layers on 4 individual plates and pour the passion fruit dressing over the top. Serve with a mixture of wild and long-grain rice with herbs tossed through.

FOOD FACT • A tropical vine fruit, passion fruit is so called because the flower of the plant is supposed to symbolize the Passion of Christ. It has a purple-brown hard skin that goes wrinkly as it ripens. The flesh is inseparable from the many tiny black edible seeds. It has an intense sharp perfume and a sweet-sour taste.

Griddled and Roasted Guinea Fowl

This is a really tasty way of serving these joints and the best way to eat them is with your fingers and lots of napkins!

Serves: **4**

Preparation time: 10 minutes

Cooking time: 45 minutes

Oven temperature: 200°C/400°F/Gas Mark 6

1.75 kg/3½ lb guinea fowl, jointed into 8 pieces
2 tablespoons Dijon mustard
grated rind and juice of 2 lemons
sea salt and pepper
grated lemon rind, to garnish

1 Heat the griddle pan. Place the guinea fowl joints on the griddle and cook all over for 25 minutes, turning frequently. The skin will become quite charred, which gives the guinea fowl a great flavour.

2 Meanwhile, mix together the Dijon mustard, lemon rind and juice and a little seasoning in a small bowl.

3 Remove the guinea fowl from the griddle pan and place in a lightly oiled roasting tin. Smear the mustard mixture all over the guinea fowl joints, using a pastry brush, and place in the top of a preheated oven, 200°C/400°F/Gas Mark 6, for 20 minutes – the mustard will form a tasty crust on the guinea fowl. To test that the meat is cooked, insert a knife into the thickest part of each joint – the juices should run clear. Serve garnished with lemon rind.

Griddled Summer Duck Salad

This is a stunning salad because of all the fantastic shades of red and the flavours, which are all so good together. If you cannot get blood oranges use tangerines instead.

Serves: **4**

Preparation time: 20 minutes

Cooking time: 25–30 minutes

2 red onions
2 red peppers, cored, deseeded and
  cut into flat pieces
4 blood oranges
4 x 200 g/7 oz duck breasts
1 bunch of dill, roughly chopped
4 tablespoons olive oil
1 tablespoon white wine vinegar
sea salt and pepper

1 Heat the griddle pan. Cut the red onions into wedges, keeping the root ends intact to hold the wedges together. Place the onions on the griddle and cook for 5 minutes on each side, or until charred and soft. Remove from the griddle and set aside.

2 Place the peppers on the griddle. Cook for 5 minutes on the skin side only, until charred and blistered. Again, remove and set aside.

3 Using a sharp knife, top and tail each orange so that it will stand on a board. Cut downwards, working around the orange, to remove the peel and pith and reveal the flesh of the orange. Cut out the orange segments between the membranes, removing any pips. Squeeze any juice left in the body of the orange.

4 Remove and discard the skin from the duck breasts. Place the duck on the griddle and cook for 4 minutes on each side for pink meat or 7 minutes for well done.

5 Mix together in a large bowl the griddled onion and pepper, the orange flesh and juice, dill, olive oil, vinegar and seasoning. Carve the griddled duck into slices when cooked. Add to the salad, mix well and serve.

Griddled Duck with Oranges and Berries

Serves: **4**

Preparation time: 10–15 minutes

Cooking time: 20 minutes

4 x 200 g/7 oz Barbary duck breasts
2 oranges
125 g/4 oz cranberries
50 g/2 oz light brown sugar
1 tablespoon honey
sea salt and pepper
250 g/8 oz cooked egg noodles, to serve
   (optional)

1 Heat the griddle pan. Using a fork, pierce the skin of the duck breasts – the more times you do it, the better the breast will be as this allows the fat to run out and make the skin crispy.

2 Place the duck breasts on the griddle, skin side down, and cook for 10 minutes. If necessary, drain off some of the cooking fat and then turn the pieces over and cook for 5 minutes on the other side.

3 Meanwhile, using a sharp knife, top and tail each orange so that it will stand on a board. Cut downwards, working all around the orange, to remove the peel and pith and reveal the flesh of the orange. Cut out the orange segments between the membranes, removing any pips. Squeeze any juice left in the body of the orange into a small saucepan.

4 Add the orange flesh, the cranberries, light brown sugar, honey and seasoning to the saucepan and simmer gently for about 4 minutes, until the cranberries are soft.

5 Remove the duck from the griddle when cooked. Carve it into slices, arrange on serving plates and serve with the orange and cranberry sauce poured over. Serve with egg noodles, if liked.

FOOD FACT • Cranberries are too acidic to be eaten raw but when cooked make ideal accompaniments for poultry and venison in particular. When buying fresh cranberries make sure they are bright, dry, plump and unshrivelled. They will keep, unwashed, in the refrigerator for up to 2 weeks. Use frozen cranberries if fresh ones are not available.

Beef, Veal & Venison

Peppered Fillet Steak

Serves: **4**

Preparation time: 15 minutes

Cooking time: 6–16 minutes

4 x 150 g/5 oz fillet steaks
4 tablespoons crushed peppercorns
2 tablespoons mustard seeds
1 teaspoon sea salt
1 egg white
TO SERVE
tomato, red onion and mozzarella salad
griddled potato wedges

1 Heat the griddle pan. Wipe the fillet steaks with kitchen paper. Mix together the crushed peppercorns, mustard seeds and sea salt and spread on a plate.

2 Tip the egg white into a dish and whisk lightly. Dip the steaks into the egg white and ensure they are well coated. Then dip the steaks into the pepper and mustard mix, rolling well to cover them all over with the spice mixture.

3 Place the steaks on the griddle and cook for 3 minutes on each side for rare, 5 minutes for medium or 8 minutes for well done. Serve with a tomato, red onion and mozzarella salad and griddled potato wedges.

FOOD FACT • Mustard seeds come from plants belonging to the cabbage family. There are three different varieties: white, brown and black mustard seeds. They have little or no smell but their hot taste is released when the seeds are crushed and moistened. White mustard seeds are in fact sand or honey coloured; they are milder and slightly larger than the other varieties.

Dry Crust Beef

Here, a dry spice rub is massaged into sirloin steak. The herbs and spices explode with flavour as they cook and give the meat a delicious crusty exterior.

Serves: **4**

Preparation time: 10 minutes

Cooking time: 12–24 minutes

1 teaspoon ground cumin
1 teaspoon allspice
1 teaspoon ground coriander
2 garlic cloves, chopped
2 bay leaves, chopped
1 teaspoon sea salt
2 teaspoons black pepper
575 g/1 lb 3 oz piece of sirloin steak
TO SERVE
4 large potatoes, baked
150 ml/¼ pint soured cream
½ red onion, finely chopped
chopped coriander
mixed leaf salad

1 Place the cumin, allspice, ground coriander, garlic, bay leaf, sea salt and pepper in a pestle and grind with the mortar.

2 Heat the griddle pan. Rub the dry ground spice mixture well into the sirloin steak, covering it all over. Place the steak on the griddle and cook for 6 minutes on each side for rare, 9 minutes for medium or 12 minutes for well done.

3 When cooked, remove the steak and allow to rest for a few minutes. Carve the steak into slices and sprinkle with any leftover dry spice mixture. Serve with crunchy-skinned baked potatoes, oozing with a mixture of soured cream, chopped red onion and fresh coriander and a mixed leaf salad.

Stuffed Fillet Steak

Serves: **4**

Preparation time: 15 minutes

Cooking time: 6–16 minutes

4 x 175 g/6 oz fillet steaks
2 garlic cloves, peeled and halved
125 g/4 oz buffalo mozzarella cheese,
  finely chopped
6 sun-dried tomatoes, chopped
1 bunch of basil, chopped
olive oil, for drizzling
sea salt and pepper
leafy green salad, to serve

1 Rub the fillet steaks all over with the halved garlic cloves. Using a sharp knife, make a slit in the side of each fillet steak and enlarge it to make a 'pocket' for the stuffing.

2 Heat the griddle pan. Mix the chopped mozzarella, sun-dried tomatoes and the basil together in a bowl with a little seasoning then use to stuff the 'pockets' in the steak. Keep any remaining mixture to use as a garnish.

3 Place the steaks on the griddle and cook for 3 minutes on each side for rare, 5 minutes for medium or 8 minutes for well done. Serve the steaks with a leafy green salad and any leftover stuffing, drizzled with a little olive oil to finish.

FOOD FACT • Mozzarella is a fresh white curd cheese, used in cooking for its texture as much as its flavour. The juices, oils and flavours of the other ingredients – in this recipe, sun-dried tomatoes and basil – are absorbed and intensified by the mild cheese. The cheese is sold swimming in whey to keep it fresh and it should be floppy rather than rubbery. Buffalo milk mozzarella is softer and more delicately flavoured than that made from cows' milk.

The Perfect Salad

One of the best accompaniments for griddled food is a fresh, well-dressed salad. The combination of smoky, firm char-grilled meat, fish or vegetables with a light, fresh, crunchy salad is unbeatable. There is an ever-increasing range of salad ingredients available, as well as a huge range of commercially available salad dressings, although it is incredibly easy to make your own at home.

Salad leaves

Lettuce is a good example of a salad ingredient that is available in an enormous array of colours, shapes and sizes, with different textures and flavours to add interest, too. When you choose a lettuce, it should be firm and crisp, with no browning on the edges and no sign of slime or insect damage. Discard any wilted outer leaves and use the lettuce within few days of purchase. Salad leaves in good condition will stay fresh for longest in the salad drawer of the refrigerator if they are placed in a plastic bag to reduce the evaporation of moisture. Leaves that have wilted can be refreshed by being plunged into cold water, shaken dry and put into the refrigerator in a plastic bag or wrapped in a damp tea towel.

Shortly before they are required, salad leaves should be washed and then thoroughly dried, by using a salad shaker or spinner, or by shaking them gently in a clean tea towel. The leaves should be torn rather than cut into bite-sized pieces, to avoid bruising.

There are various types of lettuce. Round, or cabbage, lettuces, which range in texture from soft to crisp, include Batavia, Butterhead, Quattro Stagioni and probably the most widely known variety, Iceberg which is very crisp but has little real flavour. Loosehead lettuces have no heart as such, but leaves that all splay out from the middle and are more tightly packed towards the centre. Examples are Lollo Rosso and Lollo Blondo. More elongated in shape than the round lettuce is the Cos, or Romaine, lettuce, a small variety of which is Little Gem.

There is a wide range of salad leaves besides lettuce. Examples include members of the chicory family – curly endive (frisée), escarole and radicchio – lamb's lettuce, rocket, salad burnett, baby spinach leaves and watercress. Often, you can buy bags of ready-to-eat mixed leaves, which are useful for creating an instant green salad. Fresh herbs such as basil and chives are tasty inclusions, too.

Other salad ingredients

To add colour to a green salad, add one or two of the following ingredients. Scatter whole cherry tomatoes, plump black olives, radishes or baby corn over the top, or include thinly sliced sweet mild peppers in red, yellow and orange. Red onion is another colourful addition. Mild in taste, it is ideal raw in salads, either thinly sliced into rings or finely chopped. Other more unusual option are fresh flowers, such as violets, nasturtiums and marigolds.

Salad dressings

The dressing is what really brings a salad to life, marrying all the separate ingredients into a harmonious whole. However, the best ingredients – really fresh crunchy salads and vegetables – don't need to be smothered in sauces and rich dressings. Dressings should be a light covering, not a greasy coating. This is especially true for green salads, the flavour of which is destroyed by excess vinaigrette. Remember, too, that green salads should not meet their dressings until just before serving since, once dressed, they quickly go limp. The simplest of dressings consist of little more than a good salad oil, perhaps with a little salt, a twist of freshly ground black pepper and a squeeze of lemon juice. A pinch or two of sugar can make a welcome addition, as can a teaspoon or two of mustard.

Experiment with different ingredients and quantities, however, to create your own favourite salad dressing, using a good-quality salad oil as your base. Olive oil is the best known, varying enormously in flavour and character, depending on its country of origin and the olives it is made from. Extra virgin olive oil is the best quality, having been made from the first pressing of the olives. Other salad oils include grapeseed, groundnut, sesame seed and walnut oil. Counterbalance your oil with the acidity of a little vinegar (wine, sherry, raspberry or balsamic, for example) or lime or lemon juice, and try adding various ingredients such as crushed garlic, mustard, soy sauce, maple syrup or clear honey for sweetness, cayenne pepper for spice and various fresh or dried herbs and salt and pepper.

Teriyaki Steak

Thought to have Polynesian origins, teriyaki is a popular marinade for chicken, beef and lamb. The complex flavours of soy and ginger penetrate the meat with very tasty results.

Serves: **4**

Preparation time: 5 minutes, plus marinating

Cooking time: 6–16 minutes

1 Mix together all the ingredients for the teriyaki marinade – the ginger, soy sauce, pineapple juice and crushed garlic.

2 Place the sirloin steak in a shallow dish and pour over the marinade. Turn the steak to coat it well with the marinade. Refrigerate for 24 hours, turning as frequently as possible.

3 Heat the griddle pan. Cook the steak for 3 minutes on each side for rare, 5 minutes for medium or 8 minutes for well done. Remove when cooked to your liking. Allow to rest for a few minutes, then slice thinly and serve on a bed of stir-fried noodles and vegetables.

3 cm/1¼ inch piece of fresh root ginger, peeled and finely chopped
4 tablespoons soy sauce
100 ml/3½ fl oz pineapple juice
2 garlic cloves, crushed
700 g/1 lb 7 oz thick sirloin steak
stir-fried noodles and vegetables, to serve

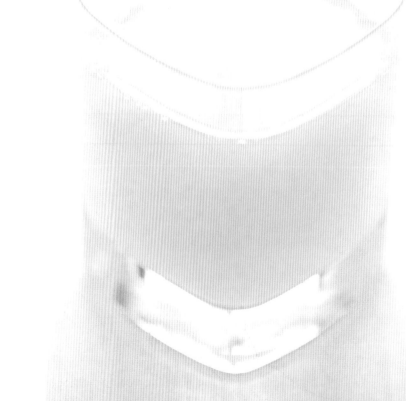

Spicy Beefburgers

These can also be made with minced lamb and served in flat Turkish bread for a change.

Serves: **4**

Preparation time: 10 minutes

Cooking time: 6–14 minutes

575 g/1 lb 3 oz lean minced beef
2 garlic cloves, crushed
1 red onion, finely chopped
1 hot red chilli, finely chopped
1 bunch of parsley, chopped
1 tablespoon Worcestershire sauce
1 egg, beaten
4 wholemeal rolls or granary buns, split
hot salad leaves, such as mizuna or rocket
1 beefsteak tomato, sliced
sea salt and pepper
TO SERVE
burger relish
Griddled New Potatoes (see page 56)
snipped chives

1 Place the minced meat in a large bowl. Add the garlic, red onion, chilli and parsley to the mince, then add the Worcestershire sauce, beaten egg and a little seasoning. Mix well.

2 Heat the griddle pan. Using your hands, divide the minced meat mixture into 4 and shape into 4 burgers. Place the burgers on the griddle and cook for 3 minutes on each side for rare, 5 minutes for medium or 7 minutes for well done.

3 Place the bun halves under a preheated hot grill and toast on one side or griddle quickly in a clean griddle pan. Fill each bun with the hot salad leaves, sliced tomato and a griddled burger, and serve with your favourite relish and griddled new potatoes, garnished with snipped chives.

Griddled Provençale Beef

Serves: **4**

Preparation time: 15 minutes

Cooking time: 10–20 minutes

575 g/1 lb 3 oz thick sirloin steak
100 g/3½ oz thin green beans, trimmed
4 beefsteak tomatoes, skinned
1 bunch of flat-leaf parsley, chopped
425 g/14 oz can butter beans, drained
100 g/3½ oz pitted olives
DRESSING
2 tablespoons Dijon mustard
6 tablespoons olive oil
2 tablespoons wine vinegar
sea salt and pepper

1 Heat the griddle pan. Place the sirloin steak on to cook – 5 minutes on each side for rare, 8 minutes for medium or 10 minutes for well-done meat.

2 Meanwhile, bring a saucepan of lightly salted water to the boil, and add the green beans. Cook for 3 minutes then refresh in cold water. When the beans are cold, drain well.

3 Cut the skinned tomatoes into wedges and remove and discard the cores and seeds. Combine the tomatoes, green beans, chopped parsley, drained butter beans and pitted olives and arrange in a serving dish.

4 To make the dressing, combine the Dijon mustard, olive oil, wine vinegar and seasoning in a small jug. Remove the steak from the griddle and leave to rest for 5 minutes before carving thinly. Arrange the pieces overlapping each other slightly on top of the salad and drizzle with the dressing.

Veal Escalopes Griddled with Dolcelatte

This makes a great, quick and tasty supper. It is an impressive dish yet very simple to make. Since veal is a pale-coloured meat it always looks particularly attractive served with a dark-coloured accompaniment such as dark green spinach or beans.

Serves: **4**

Preparation time: 10 minutes

Cooking time: 12 minutes

4 x 175 g/6 oz veal escalopes
175 g/6 oz dolcelatte cheese
200 g/7 oz bag baby spinach leaves
olive oil, for drizzling
pepper

1 Heat the griddle pan. Place the veal escalopes on the griddle and cook for 6 minutes on each side.

2 Cut the dolcelatte into thin slices and place on the top of the escalopes for the last 3 minutes of cooking.

3 Meanwhile, cook the baby spinach leaves. Place in the microwave and cook for 2 minutes on High, or empty the spinach into a wok over a high heat and stir constantly for 2 minutes. To serve, arrange the spinach on individual plates; drizzle with olive oil, season with black pepper and top with the cheesy veal escalopes.

FOOD FACT • Dolcelatte cheese is a blue veined Italian cheese which is similar to Gorgonzola cheese. It has a creamy and velvety texture and a mild, sweet taste. The translation means 'sweet milk'.

Griddled Veal Escalopes with Parsley Pesto

To make a complete meal of this, serve it with freshly cooked pasta such as penne and a large bowl of mixed green salad for a stylish and healthy meal.

Serves: **4**

Preparation time: 15 minutes

Cooking time: 10 minutes

4 x 150 g/5 oz veal escalopes

PARSLEY PESTO

1 large bunch of parsley, plus extra to garnish

100 g/3½ oz pine nuts, toasted (see page 40)

4 tablespoons olive oil

2 garlic cloves, crushed

grated rind of 2 lemons, plus extra to garnish

4 tablespoons lemon juice

sea salt and pepper

1 To make the pesto, place the parsley, pine nuts, olive oil, garlic, lemon rind and juice and a little seasoning in a blender and process until smooth.

2 Heat the griddle pan. Place the escalopes in the pan and cook for 5 minutes on each side. Serve the veal with spoonfuls of the parsley pesto to the side or on top, garnished with extra lemon rind and parsley sprigs.

Venison with Root Vegetables

Serves: **4**

Preparation time: 15 minutes

Cooking time: 25–40 minutes

Oven temperature: 200°C/400°F/Gas Mark 6

400 g/13 oz venison fillet, cut from the haunch
4 small uncooked beetroots, peeled and sliced
2 pink sweet potatoes, peeled and sliced
2 red onions
100 g/3½ oz redcurrant jelly
100 ml/3½ fl oz red wine
sea salt and pepper
chopped parsley, to garnish

1 Heat the griddle pan. Check that the venison fillet fits into the griddle pan; cut it in half to fit if necessary.

2 Place the venison fillet on the hot griddle and cook for 6 minutes on each side. Try to seal the outside evenly. Transfer the venison to a lightly oiled roasting tin and place in a preheated oven, 200°C/400°F/Gas Mark 6, to cook for a further 12–15 minutes for rare, and up to 30 minutes for well done – this depends on the thickness of the fillet.

3 Place the slices of beetroot and sweet potato in the griddle pan and cook for 8–10 minutes on each side until soft. When cooked, add them to the venison in the oven.

4 Cut the onions into wedges, keeping the root ends intact to hold the wedges together. Griddle for 6 minutes on each side. Meanwhile, place the redcurrant jelly, red wine and a little seasoning in a small saucepan and heat gently to melt the redcurrant jelly.

5 Remove the venison from the oven and leave to rest for a few minutes before carving. Add any juices from the meat to the redcurrant jelly sauce.

6 Arrange the griddled onions, beetroot and sweet potatoes on 4 plates. Top with slices of venison and drizzle the sauce over the top. Garnish with chopped parsley and serve.

Mixed Pepper-crusted Venison

Serves: **4**

Preparation time: 10 minutes

Cooking time: 25–40 minutes

Oven temperature: 200°C/400°F/Gas Mark 6

750 g/1½ lb venison fillet, cut from the haunch
75 g/3 oz mixed peppercorns, crushed
25 g/1 oz juniper berries, crushed
1 egg white
sea salt
chives, to garnish
TO SERVE
redcurrant jelly
sweet potato chips

1 Heat the griddle pan. Check that the venison fillet fits into the griddle pan; cut it in half to fit if necessary.

2 Mix the peppercorns and juniper berries together with a little salt, and place in a large shallow dish. Tip the egg white into another shallow dish and whisk lightly. Dip the venison into the egg white, then roll it in the peppercorn mix, covering the meat all over with an even layer of the crust ingredients.

3 Cook the venison on the griddle for 4 minutes on each side, turning it carefully so that the crust stays intact. Cook evenly on all sides, then transfer the venison to a lightly oiled roasting tin and cook in a preheated oven, 200°C/400°F/Gas Mark 6, for a further 15 minutes for rare, and up to 30 minutes for well done – this depends on the thickness of the fillet. Slice the meat thinly.

4 Serve the venison, garnished with chives and accompanied by redcurrant jelly and finely sliced sweet potato chips.

FOOD FACT • Juniper berries are primarily used for making gin. However, they also add a subtle yet spicy flavour when combined with venison, beef, rabbit and pork. They can be added to marinades, terrines and stuffings.

Pork & Lamb

Asian Pork Cakes

Make a meal of these tasty pork cakes by serving with plain boiled rice and Chilli Jam (see page 146) for dipping.

Serves: **4**

Preparation time: 20 minutes

Cooking time: 30 minutes

575 g/1 lb 3 oz minced pork
4 cm/1½ inch piece of galangal, finely chopped
4 garlic cloves, finely chopped
1 bunch of coriander, finely chopped
1 lemon grass stalk, finely chopped
2 chillies, finely chopped
1 tablespoon Thai fish sauce
1 egg, beaten
griddled chillies and lemon grass, to garnish

1 Place the minced pork in a bowl. Add to it the finely chopped galangal, garlic, coriander, lemon grass and chillies, the fish sauce and the beaten egg; mix well.

2 Heat the griddle pan. Divide the pork mixture into 12. Using your hands, shape into balls and then flatten slightly to make 'cakes'. If the mixture sticks to your hands, try dipping your hands in cold water before forming the pork cakes.

3 Cook the pork cakes in batches on the griddle for 6 minutes on each side, keeping cooked ones warm in the oven while you cook the remainder.

4 Pile the pork cakes on a serving dish and garnish with griddled chillies and lemon grass.

FOOD FACT • Lemon grass is a tall, hard grass with pale green leaves, which have a distinctive lemony aroma and taste. It is most often used in south-east Asian cooking. Often, the stems are bruised before use in order to release their flavour, then added whole before cooking and removed prior to serving. Alternatively, the tender inner leaves are chopped, shredded or ground and used as a flavouring. Lemon grass is best fresh but can also be bought dried, in which case it needs soaking for 30 minutes before use. Fresh lemon grass keeps well for several weeks wrapped in newspaper in the vegetable drawer of the refrigerator.

Pork Fillet with Apricots

Serves: **4**

Preparation time: 15 minutes

Cooking time: 35 minutes

Oven temperature: 180°C/350°F/Gas Mark 4

700 g/1 lb 7 oz pork fillet
2 red onions
8 apricots, halved and stoned
1 bunch of thyme
4 tablespoons olive oil
1 tablespoon cider vinegar
sea salt and pepper
spiced rice, to serve

1 Heat the griddle pan. Slice the pork fillet into 2.5 cm/1 inch rounds. Cook on the griddle for 7–8 minutes on each side, then remove, place in an ovenproof dish and transfer to a preheated oven, 180ºC/350ºF/Gas Mark 4.

2 Cut the red onions into wedges, keeping the root ends intact to hold the wedges together, and cook on the griddle for 5 minutes on each side. Add to the pork in the oven.

3 Place the apricot halves on the griddle and cook for 5 minutes on each side. Add the thyme leaves for the last minute of cooking, then transfer everything to the oven.

4 Mix together the olive oil, cider vinegar and a little seasoning. Drizzle over the griddled ingredients and serve the pork with rice spiced with garlic, turmeric, curry powder or paprika.

Pork Steaks with Griddled Vegetables

This dish is ideal served with freshly cooked egg tagliatelle, tossed in olive oil and seasoning.

Serves: **4**

Preparation time: 15 minutes

Cooking time: 30 minutes

Oven temperature: 200°C/400°F/Gas Mark 6

2 yellow peppers, quartered, cored and deseeded
2 red peppers, quartered, cored and deseeded
2 courgettes, sliced
2 red onions
1 bunch of sage, roughly chopped, plus extra to garnish
4 x 150 g/5 oz pork steaks
1 garlic clove, peeled and halved
dash of white wine
sea salt and pepper

1 Heat the griddle pan. Place peppers on the griddle and cook for 6 minutes on the skin side and 3 minutes on the other. Remove to a large ovenproof dish and place in a preheated oven, 200°C/400°F/Gas Mark 6.

2 Add the courgette slices to the griddle and cook for 2 minutes on each side. Remove from the pan and add to the peppers in the oven.

3 Cut the red onions into wedges, keeping the root ends intact to hold the wedges together. Add to the griddle and cook for 4 minutes on each side. Add half of the roughly chopped sage to the onions for the last minute of cooking. Mix the griddled sage and onions in with the other vegetables in the oven.

4 Take the pork steaks and rub them all over with the halved clove of garlic. Place the pork steaks on the griddle and cook for 6 minutes on each side. Remove from the pan when cooked and add the pork to the vegetables in the oven.

5 Finally, add the remaining sage, a dash of white wine and a little seasoning to the griddle pan. Bring to the boil.

6 To serve, arrange the griddled vegetables on individual plates topped with the pork. Drizzle over the wine and sage sauce and serve garnished with sage leaves.

Griddled Sausages and Vegetable Polenta

This dish brings a whole new meaning to 'sausages for supper'. Serve it to your friends and they will think that you have a chef in the kitchen!

Serves: **4**

Preparation time: 10 minutes

Cooking time: 1 hour

Oven temperature: 180ºC/350ºF/Gas Mark 4

FOOD FACT • Polenta is the name of both the cornmeal ground from sweetcorn or maize, and the name of the traditional north Italian dish made using coarsely ground cornmeal. The latter is made by first boiling the cornmeal until porridge-like. It is then either served soft or allowed to set before being sliced and fried, grilled or griddled, as here.

600 ml/1 pint boiling water
150 g/5 oz polenta
2 garlic cloves, crushed
8 speciality sausages
2 red onions
2 leeks, sliced
2 red peppers, cored, deseeded and cut into flat pieces
2 large mushrooms, quartered
4 tablespoons olive oil
4 teaspoons sherry vinegar
75 g/3 oz Parmesan cheese shavings
sea salt and pepper

1 Set a saucepan containing the boiling water on the stove over a medium heat. Pour in the polenta and stir well until smooth. Add the crushed garlic. Reduce the heat and allow to simmer for 5 minutes, stirring frequently, until the mixture becomes stiff and hard to work.

2 Heat the griddle pan. Remove the polenta from the pan, spread on a lightly oiled chopping board and set aside.

3 Place the sausages on the griddle and cook for 10 minutes, turning them to seal the outsides. When cooked, place in a roasting tin in a preheated oven, 180ºC/350ºF/Gas Mark 4.

4 Cut the onions into wedges, keeping the root ends intact to hold the wedges together. Cook on the griddle for 4 minutes on each side, then remove and add to the sausages in the oven. Griddle the leeks for 4 minutes on each side, then place in the oven, too.

5 Place the peppers on the griddle and cook for 5 minutes on the skin side only, until the skin blisters. Place them in the tin in the oven.

6 Cook the mushroom quarters on the griddle for 4 minutes on each side, cooking them gills facing down first, then add to the other griddled ingredients in the roasting tin.

7 Cut the set polenta into 4 pieces. Place on the griddle and cook for 5 minutes on each side over a high heat. Serve the griddled polenta arranged on individual plates and topped with the griddled vegetables and the sausages. Drizzle over the olive oil combined with the sherry vinegar and sprinkle with the Parmesan shavings and a little salt and pepper.

Italian Sausages and Penne

This deliciously easy dish is great for the family or for informal entertaining. Speciality sausages are very popular – check out your local supermarket or butcher to find some great spicy Italian sausages.

Serves: **4**

Preparation time: 10 minutes

Cooking time: 50 minutes

8 Italian sausages
2 courgettes, thinly sliced
2 red onions
400 g/13 oz penne
300 g/10 oz broccoli florets
2 tablespoons chilli oil
100 g/3½ oz Parmesan cheese, freshly grated
chopped sage, to serve

1 Heat the griddle pan. Cook the sausages for 25 minutes, turning them constantly to achieve a good even colour. When cooked, remove from the griddle and keep warm in a low oven.

2 Cook the courgette slices on the griddle for 2 minutes on each side. Remove and keep warm. Cut the onions into slim wedges, keeping the root ends intact to hold the wedges together. Place on the griddle and cook for 5 minutes on each side.

3 Meanwhile, bring a large saucepan of lightly salted water to the boil. When boiling, plunge the penne into the water and cook for 12 minutes, or according to packet instructions. Add the broccoli florets for the last 2 minutes of cooking.

4 Drain the pasta and broccoli well. Tip into a serving bowl and add the chilli oil and grated Parmesan. Slice the cooked sausages and add to the pasta together with the griddled vegetables. Mix well, stir through some chopped sage and serve.

Gammon with Honey and Nut Sauce

Serves: **4**

Preparation time: 10 minutes

Cooking time: 20 minutes

4 x 175 g/6 oz gammon steaks
4 tablespoons honey
125 g/4 oz cashew nuts, roughly chopped
2 tablespoons dry sherry
1 teaspoon paprika
salad, to serve

1 Heat the griddle pan. Place the gammon steaks on the griddle and cook for 10 minutes on each side.

2 Meanwhile, gently warm the honey in a small saucepan and add the roughly chopped cashew nuts, the dry sherry and paprika. Allow to simmer for 5 minutes.

3 When the gammon is cooked, cut the steaks into long strips, place in a serving dish and spoon over the honey and nut sauce. Serve with a fresh salad.

FOOD FACT • Cashews are kidney-shaped nuts, always sold shelled because their shells are toxic. They are usually used plain for cooking, but are also available roasted or salted and are popular appetizers with drinks. Cashews have a slightly crumbly texture and delicate sweet flavour.

Liver, Bacon and Kidney with Rosemary Onions

This is a popular meal with those who love velvety lambs' liver, juicy kidneys and sizzling bacon. It's so easy to cook, too, and especially great served with creamy mashed potatoes with a spoonful of English mustard added.

4 kidneys
2 onions
4 smoked back or streaky bacon rashers
1 rosemary sprig, chopped
4 x 125 g/4 oz thin slices of lambs' liver
olive oil, for drizzling
sea salt and pepper

Serves: **4**

Preparation time: 10 minutes

Cooking time: 20 minutes

1 Heat the griddle pan. Cut the kidneys in half and cut away any white tissues and fat. Cut the onions into wedges, keeping the root ends intact to hold the wedges together.

2 Place the kidneys on the griddle, together with the bacon and onions. Cook the meat for 4–5 minutes on each side; when cooked remove and keep warm in a low oven.

3 Add the rosemary to the onions and push them to the side of the pan. Place the slices of liver on the griddle and cook for 3–5 minutes on each side. You will need to cook the liver in batches, so cook any well-done requests first and keep these warm, cooking the rarer requests last. Keep turning the onions to ensure even colouring all over.

4 Serve the griddled liver, bacon and kidney with the rosemary onions, drizzled with a little olive oil, and sprinkled with salt and pepper.

Griddled Bacon and Butternut Squash Pasta

You can peel the squash before slicing it if you prefer, or leave the skin on and eat it – all the vitamins are just below the skin.

Serves: **4**

Preparation time: 10 minutes

Cooking time: 40 minutes

Oven temperature: 200°C/400°F/Gas Mark 6

½ butternut squash
2 onions, sliced
16 back bacon rashers
300 g/10 oz penne
1 bunch of chives, chopped
pumpkin oil, for drizzling
sea salt and pepper

1 Heat the griddle pan. Remove the seeds from the squash and slice the flesh into slim wedges. Place on the griddle to cook for 12 minutes on each side. Remove from the griddle, put in a roasting tin and place in a preheated oven, 200°C/400°F/Gas Mark 6.

2 Griddle the sliced onions for 4 minutes on each side. When the onions are cooked, add them to the pumpkin in the oven. Add the bacon to the griddle and cook for 4 minutes on each side.

3 Meanwhile, bring a large saucepan of lightly salted water to the boil. When boiling, plunge the penne into the water and cook for 12 minutes, or according to packet instructions.

4 Drain the cooked pasta well. Tip into a large bowl. Cut the cooked bacon into strips and add to the pasta with the griddled pumpkin and onion, the chopped chives and a little seasoning. Mix together and serve drizzled with a little pumpkin oil.

FOOD FACT • Made from roasted pumpkin seeds, pumpkin oil is dark brown in colour. It has a strong nutty flavour, similar to sesame seed oil, and should be used sparingly. It is best used as a salad dressing, in mayonnaise or drizzled over cooked dishes, as here, rather than for cooking. Pumpkin oil is available from any good delicatessen.

Lamb Fillet with Wholegrain Mustard Crust and Roasted Tomatoes

This delicious dish is a little expensive since it uses loin of lamb fillet, which is the best cut, but it is worth every penny since there is no wastage.

Serves: **4**

Preparation time: 15 minutes

Cooking time: 20–40 minutes

575 g/1 lb 3 oz loin of lamb fillet
1 rosemary sprig, broken into short lengths
2 garlic cloves, peeled and sliced
4 tablespoons wholegrain mustard
750 g/1½ lb small vine tomatoes, roasted (see below)
200 g/7 oz wild rocket
4 tablespoons olive oil
2 tablespoons balsamic vinegar
sea salt and pepper

1 Heat the griddle pan. Cut the lamb into 2 lengths so that it will fit in the pan. Using a small sharp knife, make holes in the lamb and insert pieces of rosemary and slices of garlic into the slits. Spread the wholegrain mustard all over the lamb.

2 Place the lamb on the griddle and cook, turning it halfway through cooking, for a total of 20 minutes for rare, 30 minutes for medium or 40 minutes for well done.

3 Arrange the roasted vine tomatoes and wild rocket on individual plates. When the lamb is cooked, remove from the griddle pan and allow to rest for a few minutes before carving. Slice into 5 mm/¼ inch rounds and arrange on the plates with the salad. Drizzle with olive oil and balsamic vinegar, and sprinkle with salt and pepper before serving.

FOOD FACT • To roast tomatoes, choose small tomatoes on the vine and simply place them on a roasting tin in a preheated oven, 110°C/225°F/Gas Mark ¼, for up to 4 hours. The longer you cook them, the sweeter and more intense in flavour the tomatoes become.

Lamb and Haloumi Kebabs with Mint and Tomato Salad

Serves: **4**

Preparation time: 10 minutes

Cooking time: 20–25 minutes

400 g/13 oz lamb fillet
250 g/8 oz haloumi cheese, sliced
1 aubergine
mint sprigs, to garnish
MINT AND TOMATO SALAD
1 red onion
4 beefsteak tomatoes, skinned and sliced
1 bunch of mint, chopped
4 tablespoons olive oil
1 tablespoon white wine vinegar
sea salt and pepper

1 Trim the lamb of any excess fat and slice the fillet into 3 cm/1¼ inch rounds. Cut each slice of haloumi in half. Cut the aubergine into chunks of a similar size to the lamb and cheese. Thread the pieces of lamb, haloumi and aubergine alternately on to 8 presoaked wooden skewers which fit in the griddle pan.

2 Heat the griddle pan. When hot, add the kebabs and cook on all sides for a total of 20–25 minutes.

3 Meanwhile, make the salad. Peel the red onion and slice it very finely, preferably using a mandolin. Chop the onion slices into small dice. Place in a bowl with the sliced tomatoes, the chopped mint, olive oil, vinegar and seasoning. Mix well, arrange on individual plates or in a serving bowl and serve with the lamb and haloumi kebabs, garnished with mint.

FOOD FACT • Haloumi is a traditional stretched curd cheese, which is shiny white and smooth and comes in rectangular blocks or loaf shapes. Originally a sheep's or goats' milk cheese from Cyprus, it is now more widely produced, often from cows' milk. Haloumi has a rubbery texture and is basically a cooking cheese, which holds its shape when fried or grilled. The outside becomes crisp while the inside melts, like mozzarella.

Japanese Lamb Chops with Cucumber Salad

Serves: **4**

Preparation time: 10 minutes, plus marinating

Cooking time: 8–16 minutes

8 x 75–125 g/3–4 oz lamb chops
MARINADE
4 tablespoons soy sauce
4 tablespoons mirin
4 tablespoons sake
1 garlic clove, crushed
6 cm/2½ inch piece of fresh root ginger,
  finely chopped
CUCUMBER SALAD
1 cucumber
2 tablespoons rice vinegar
1 tablespoon vegetable oil
sea salt and pepper

1 Combine all the marinade ingredients in a shallow dish. Add the chops and turn them to cover completely in the marinade. Cover the dish with clingfilm and leave the lamb to marinate at room temperature for 2 hours.

2 To make the cucumber salad, grate the cucumber into a bowl. Add the rice vinegar, vegetable oil and a little seasoning. Mix well.

3 Heat the griddle pan. Cook the marinated lamb chops for 4 minutes on each side for rare, 5 minutes for medium or 8 minutes for well done. Arrange the chops on 4 individual plates and serve with the cucumber salad.

FOOD FACT • Mirin is a very sweet, thick, amber-coloured Japanese rice wine, used for seasoning, in marinades and for basting. Sake is thought of as a rice wine, too, but is actually derived from a method more related to brewing than to wine-making, whereby yeast is added to rice after it has boiled. Sake is a colourless liquid and, like mirin, is often used in marinades in Japanese cooking.

Harissa

If you like your food spicy, this 'Moroccan mayonnaise' is an ideal accompaniment for meat, such as Moroccan Lamb (see page 228), and fish dishes. You can also add it to soups, spread it on bread or serve it as a salad dressing.

Makes: **1 jar**

Preparation time: 10 minutes

Cooking time: 25 minutes

4 red peppers
4 large red chillies
2 garlic cloves, crushed
½ teaspoon coriander seeds
1 teaspoon caraway seeds
5 tablespoons olive oil

1 Heat the griddle pan. Add the whole red peppers and cook for 15 minutes, turning occasionally. The skins will blacken and start to lift. Place the peppers in a plastic bag, seal the bag and set aside for a while. Sealing the griddled peppers in plastic encourages them to 'sweat', which makes it easier to remove their skins. When cool enough to handle, remove the skin, cores and seeds from the peppers and place the flesh in a blender or food processor.

2 Remove the skin, cores and seeds from the red chillies in the same way and place the chilli flesh in the blender, together with the garlic, coriander and caraway seeds and olive oil. Process in the blender to a smooth paste.

3 If not required immediately, place the harissa in a sealable container and pour a thin layer of olive oil over the top. Cover with a lid and refrigerate.

FOOD FACT • There are dozens of varieties of chillies. These range from mildly warm to blisteringly hot and can vary in length from 5 mm/¼ inch to 30 cm/12 inches. Fresh chillies should look bright and shiny, with no markings on the skin. Capsaicin is the oil found in the seeds and ribs of chillies that accounts for the heat. Capsaicin is an irritant, so take great care not to touch eyes and lips after handling chillies. To prepare chillies, pull off their stalks and cut them in half lengthways. Do this under cold running water to prevent irritating fumes rising into your face. Whether you remove the seeds or not depends on personal preference.

Moroccan Lamb

Serves: **4**

Preparation time: 15 minutes

Cooking time: 1 hour

1 kg/2 lb boned leg of lamb
2 garlic cloves, crushed
1 teaspoon paprika
1 teaspoon ground cumin
1 teaspoon ground coriander
1 teaspoon ground ginger
1 teaspoon ground cinnamon
good pinch of dried chilli flakes
coriander sprigs, to garnish
TO SERVE
Harissa (see page 226)
Moroccan Griddled Vegetable Salad
   (see page 20)

1 Trim the lamb of any excess fat. Mix the crushed garlic with the spices and rub the mixture all over the lamb, covering all the surfaces of the meat well with the spices.

2 Heat the griddle pan. Place the lamb on the griddle and cook for 30 minutes on each side. Begin with the griddle very hot so as to seal the meat, then lower the heat so that the outside of the meat does not become too blackened.

3 Remove the lamb and allow to rest for 5 minutes before carving. Garnish with coriander sprigs and serve with harissa and moroccan griddled vegetable salad, if liked.

Griddled Chump Chops with Oregano Salsa

Serves: **4**

Preparation time: 10 minutes

Cooking time: 30 minutes

4 x 200–250 g/7–8 oz chump lamb chops
4 beefsteak tomatoes, skinned
1 red onion, chopped
1 garlic clove, crushed¯
1 bunch of oregano, chopped, plus extra
  to garnish
4 tablespoons olive oil
sea salt and pepper

1 Heat the griddle pan. Place the chump chops on to cook for 15 minutes on each side.

2 Make a salsa by cutting the skinned tomatoes into wedges and removing and discarding the cores and seeds. Chop the remaining tomato flesh and mix in a bowl with the chopped red onion and crushed garlic.

3 Add the oregano to the salsa, together with the olive oil and a little seasoning. Mix well and leave for all the flavours to blend. Check that the chump chops are cooked and serve with the salsa, garnished with oregano.

FOOD FACT • To skin tomatoes, cut a cross in each using a sharp knife. Place them in a bowl and pour in enough boiling water to cover. Leave for a few minutes, then drain. The skin will have started to lift up where cut and you should now be able to remove the skins from the tomatoes quite easily.

Sweet Delights

Hot Griddled Fruit Salad

This is a great way of serving fruit as the sweetness really sings through. Children, in particular, seem to love the sweetness of griddled fruit. If you like the aromatic flavour of cardamom, try sprinkling over a few seeds to decorate.

Serves: **4**

Preparation time: 15 minutes

Cooking time: 30 minutes

1 small pineapple
1 mango
1 nectarine, quartered and stoned
1 peach, quartered and stoned
2 apricots, halved, or quartered if large, and stoned
4 tablespoons Greek yogurt
clear honey, for drizzling

1 To prepare the pineapple, top and tail it and place it on one end on a chopping board. Using a sharp knife, cut downwards to remove the skin, working all around the pineapple. Cut the pineapple flesh into chunks – in a small pineapple the core is usually sweet and soft enough to eat.

2 Heat the griddle pan. Using a sharp knife, peel the mango and cut it into slices either side of the stone. Place the mango slices on the griddle and cook for 4 minutes on each side. Remove from the griddle and set aside.

3 Place the pineapple chunks on the griddle and cook for 4 minutes on each side, then remove and set aside.

4 Place the nectarine and peach quarters on the griddle and cook for 3 minutes on each side. Remove from the griddle and set aside, then place the apricot pieces in the pan. Griddle these for 3 minutes on each side.

5 To serve, arrange the griddled fruit in individual serving dishes. Top each with a tablespoonful of Greek yogurt and drizzle clear honey over the top.

FOOD FACT • Pineapple has a high sugar content and makes an excellent dessert fruit. Small pineapples often have a more delicate flavour than large ones. When buying a pineapple, choose one that is fully ripe and fragrant – you should be able to pull out a central leaf easily from the top of the fruit. Avoid pineapples with a discoloured stalk end or wilting leaves. Soft dark patches on the flesh indicate bruising.

Griddled Pancakes with Ice Cream and Maple Syrup

Serves: **4**

Preparation time: 10 minutes

Cooking time: 6 minutes

1 large egg
3 dessertspoons vegetable oil
75 g/3 oz self-raising flour
15 g/½ oz sugar
150 ml/¼ pint milk
8 scoops of ice cream
bottled maple syrup, to serve

1 To make the pancake batter, place the egg, oil, flour, sugar and milk in a food processor or blender and process until a smooth creamy consistency is reached. Alternatively, beat together in a mixing bowl until smooth.

2 Heat the griddle pan to a medium heat and place a small pool of the batter in each corner of the griddle, to make 4 pancakes.

3 After about 1 minute, the bottoms of the pancakes will form a crust, the tops will start to set and air bubbles will rise. Using a spatula, carefully turn the pancakes over and cook on the other side for 1 minute.

4 Repeat twice more until all the batter is used – making 12 cakes in all. Serve 3 of the small pancakes per person, with scoops of ice cream and maple sauce drizzled over the top.

Griddled Apples with Cinnamon Ice Cream

In order to prevent cut apples from turning brown, dip the cut pieces in lemon juice and pat dry with kitchen towel before griddling.

Serves: **4**

Preparation time: 5 minutes

Cooking time: 12–16 minutes

4 braeburn apples
cinnamon ice cream
spun sugar, to decorate (optional)

1 Heat the griddle pan. Cut the apples into quarters and remove the cores. Cut each quarter in half again to create 8 wedges from each apple. Place on the griddle and cook for 3–4 minutes on each side.

2 Remove the apples from the griddle and place in a serving bowl or on individual plates. Serve with generous scoops of ice cream and decorate with spun sugar, if using.

FOOD FACT • Braeburn apples are red flushed and striped over greenish yellow. With crisp to firm flesh and a refreshing, fruity taste, braeburns are widely available almost all year round. A suitable alternative for this recipe would be coxes or any other seasonal dessert apple.

Griddled Mango with Fresh Lime Juice

Make this dessert when mangoes are in season and therefore inexpensive so you can decadently eat as many as you wish!

Serves: **4**

Preparation time: 10 minutes

Cooking time: 10 minutes

4 mangos
2 limes, cut into wedges
lime zest, to decorate
Greek yogurt, to serve (optional)

1 Heat the griddle pan. Using a sharp knife remove the skin from the mangoes and cut each one into thick slices, either side of the stone. Place the mango slices on the griddle and cook for 5 minutes on each side.

2 Arrange on serving plates and serve with wedges of lime, to be squeezed over just before eating. Decorate with lime zest and serve with a dollop of Greek yogurt, if liked.

A Flavour of Fruit

An excellent variety of fresh fruit, both local and imported tropical produce, is now on sale all year round and the availability of tasty organic fruits, grown without the use of chemicals, continues to improve. New fruit varieties are continually appearing, with the continuous development of cross-hybrids. And, as with vegetables, there is also a trend towards developing baby fruits such as baby pineapples, pears and dwarf bananas.

Griddling fruit is a fairly new idea, but a great way of producing a quick, yet elegant dessert. The sugars in the fruit caramelize during cooking, concentrating the flavours and making them sweeter than ever.

Choosing and storing fruit

Choose fruits that look bright and fresh and avoid any with bruised or shrivelled skins or soft spots. If possible, buy fruit that is displayed openly rather than prepackaged. In general, fruit should feel heavy for its size, which indicates a good moisture content.

Some varieties of fruit are more delicate than others, but they all need careful handling to avoid bruising. Fully ripe fruit should be used as soon as possible. It varies with individual fruit as to how to test for ripeness. However, fragrant fruits, such as melons, mangoes, pineapples and peaches all have a distinctive aroma when ripe, which is a useful tell-tale sign. Similarly, apples are fragrant when ripe and should be firm. Most ripe fruits, including soft fruit,

peaches, apricots, plums and tropical fruits should be stored in the refrigerator, while under-ripe fruit and bananas should be stored at room temperature. Most unripe fruits will eventually ripen at home at room temperature, although some, such as melons and peaches, will never do so if they have been picked way too early.

Preparing fruit

Most fruits are straightforward to prepare. There are, however, some useful tips for removing stones. For peaches, apricots or nectarines, find the natural indentation in the fruit and cut around the flesh along this line, through to the stone. Then twist the two halves apart. For plums, cut around the 'waist' of the plum, i.e. across the indentation, before twisting the two halves apart.

To stone a mango, remove a thick slice from either side of the fruit, cutting as close to the stone as possible. Remove the flesh left surrounding the stone, using a sharp knife, and cut it into cubes. If you want to cube the two thick slices of mango, score each slice into squares, cutting down to the skin but not through it. Push the skin inside out, so that the cubes can be easily sliced away from the curving skin.

To core pears, it is easier to cut them in half or into quarters lengthways first. You can then see the core to remove it, which ensures that no flesh is wasted. Apples can be cored in the

same way as pears.

Once you have peeled a pineapple (see page 234) you may want to create neat-looking pineapple rings ready for griddling. Make these by using small metal pastry or biscuit cutters. First cut the pineapple into round slices. Then use a small cutter to remove the hard central core from each slice and a larger one almost the size of the pineapple slice, with which to 'stamp out' a pineapple ring with a neat, round edge. Smaller pineapples and baby varieties do not need to be cored in this way as the central portion is tender enough to eat. Just slice them and neaten up the outside edges, if wished.

Griddling fruit

Griddling enhances the aroma and sweetness of the many varieties of fruit that take naturally to the griddle. Fruits suited to griddling include orchard fruits, such as apples, pears, plums, nectarines, apricots and peaches; some tropical fruit such as bananas, pineapples and mangoes, and others such as cherries, fresh figs and tangerines. Most fruits can be griddled with the peel left on, although pineapple is an exception.

If you like, some fruits can be marinated in red or white wine, to which chopped fresh mint has been added, before griddling. Or try marinating peach or apricot halves in brandy for 30 minutes before griddling.

As with vegetables, choose fruits that are in good, firm condition so that they don't fall apart when cooked – pay particular attention to this when it comes to bananas. For this reason, use crisp-textured dessert apples for griddling, as opposed to cooking apples, which would go mushy. Griddle your chosen fruit for a few minutes only – just long enough to bring out the aroma and flavour of the fruit being griddled.

Serving suggestions

Simple accompaniments for griddled fruits are the best. Try serving griddled fruits with a spoonful of mascarpone sprinkled with a sweet spice such as cinnamon or allspice. Alternatives include a cream sauce flavoured with chocolate or a liqueur, or a spoonful of luxury ice cream or frozen yogurt. Griddled fruits, such as apples, pears and figs, go well served with an assortment of fresh or even griddled cheese. Other possible accompaniments are slices of griddled brioche, panettone or currant bread.

Instead of griddling fruit simply in slices or cubes, why not try making fruit kebabs? Thread strawberries on to presoaked wooden skewers, or use chunks of exotic fruit such as mangoes, pineapple and kiwi fruit. Cook on the griddle and serve them still skewered, with one of the above accompaniments.

Griddled Pineapple with Fresh Coconut

Serves: **4**

Preparation time: 10 minutes

Cooking time: 16–20 minutes

1 pineapple
white flesh of ½ coconut
2 tablespoons dark or white rum
200 ml/7 fl oz double cream, whipped, to serve
light soft brown sugar, for sprinkling (optional)

1 Heat the griddle pan. Top and tail the pineapple, then place it on one end on a chopping board and, using a sharp knife, cut downwards to remove the skin, working all around the pineapple (see page 234). Cut the pineapple in half lengthways, remove the core and slice the flesh into 3 cm/1¼ inch widths and then into chunks.

2 Place the pineapple on the griddle and cook in batches for 3–4 minutes on each side.

3 Slice the coconut into very thin slithers, add to the griddle and cook for 1 minute on each side.

4 To serve, divide the pineapple between 4 dishes. Sprinkle over the griddled coconut, followed by a little rum. Serve with whipped cream sprinkled with brown sugar, if liked.

FOOD FACT • When buying a coconut, shake it to test for freshness – you will be able to hear the liquid – and ensure there is no mould around the three 'eyes'. To prepare a fresh coconut, puncture two of the 'eyes', using a hammer and screwdriver, and drain out the coconut milk. To crack open the shell, tap around the widest part with a hammer to find the nut's natural fault line. Once a crack appears in the shell, continue turning and tapping the coconut to make a clean break. Separate the halves and prise the coconut flesh from the shell with a sharp knife.

Panettone with Griddled Peaches

Serves: **4**

Preparation time: 10 minutes

Cooking time: 10 minutes

4 slices of panettone
4 peaches, halved and stoned
50 g/2 oz ground almonds
25 g/1 oz brown sugar
200 ml/7 fl oz mascarpone cheese
clear honey, for drizzling

1 Heat the griddle pan. Place the slices of panettone on the griddle and cook for 4 minutes on each side. Remove and keep warm.

2 Cut the peach halves into 4 and add the peach wedges to the griddle. Cook for 3 minutes on each side, or until coloured.

3 Meanwhile, place the ground almonds in a small bowl, add the brown sugar and mascarpone cheese. Mix together well.

4 To serve, place a slice of griddled panettone in each of 4 dishes. Place the mascarpone mixture and the griddled peaches on top. Drizzle with a little honey and serve.

FOOD FACT • Mascarpone is a very rich, creamy and mild-tasting Italian soft cheese made from fresh cream. It is often used in desserts – notably tiramisu – flavoured with liqueurs and powdered coffee and chocolate, and may also be an ingredient in creamy pasta sauces. Panettone is an Italian spiced sweet bread, traditionally eaten at Christmas, which contains dried fruit. The name comes from the Italian for a small loaf, *panetto*.

Griddled Strawberries on Ice Cream

Ice cream topped with hot sauces or fruits is unbeatable and what better than beautiful strawberries when in season? This recipe works equally well with fresh cherries or plums.

Serves: **4**

Preparation time: 5 minutes

Cooking time: 3–4 minutes

500 g/1 lb strawberries, washed but unhulled
500 ml/17 fl oz carton luxury ice cream (such as vanilla, strawberry or chocolate), to serve

1 Heat the griddle pan. Place the strawberries on the griddle and cook for 3–4 minutes, turning frequently.

2 While they are cooking, spoon scoops of luxury ice cream into 4 serving dishes. Spoon the griddled strawberries on top and serve.

Griddled Bananas with Fruit Sauce and Ice Cream

Serves: **4**

Preparation time: 10 minutes

Cooking time: 25 minutes

4 bananas
vanilla ice cream, to serve
FRUIT SAUCE
200 g/7 oz dried peaches or apricots
200 ml/7 fl oz pineapple juice
1 teaspoon cinnamon

1 To make the sauce, place the peaches or apricots, pineapple juice and cinnamon in a saucepan and bring to the boil. Reduce the heat and simmer for 10 minutes, or until the fruits are soft. Cool slightly, then place in a blender and process until smooth.

2 Heat the griddle pan. Place the bananas on the griddle whole and cook them for about 12 minutes, turning them to allow the skins to go completely black.

3 Peel the bananas. Serve each with scoops of vanilla ice cream and spoonfuls of the sauce.

Index

Acknowledgments

Photo Credits
Special photography by Sean Myers

Jacket photography by Sean Myers, David Loftus and Neil Mersh

All other photography
Octopus Publishing Group Ltd./Philip Webb

Special photograhpy Home economist
Eliza Baird